Affinity Publisher 2.0 For Book Formatting Part 1

AFFINITY PUBLISHER 2.0 FOR
SELF-PUBLISHING - BOOK 1

M.L. HUMPHREY

SELECT TITLES BY M.L. HUMPHREY

CONTENTS

CONTENTS (CONT.)

CONTENTS (CONT.)

INTRODUCTION

This book is meant to teach you how to use Affinity Publisher 2.0 to format the interior of a basic print title that uses a small accent image. We will walk through from start to finish how to create your master pages, how to build your document, how to add text, how to format that text, etc. all the way through to how to generate the finished PDF for upload to KDP Print, IngramSpark, or any other printer you may want to use.

Before we begin, though, it is important that you know which version of Affinity you are using, because some of the options we're going to discuss here, such as studios and panels, were moved around in Affinity Publisher 2.0 compared to the original Affinity Publisher.

HOW TO TELL YOUR AFFINITY VERSION

I am working on a Windows computer and there Affinity Publisher 2.0 is shown as Affinity Publisher 2, whereas the original program shows as just Affinity Publisher, as you can see here:

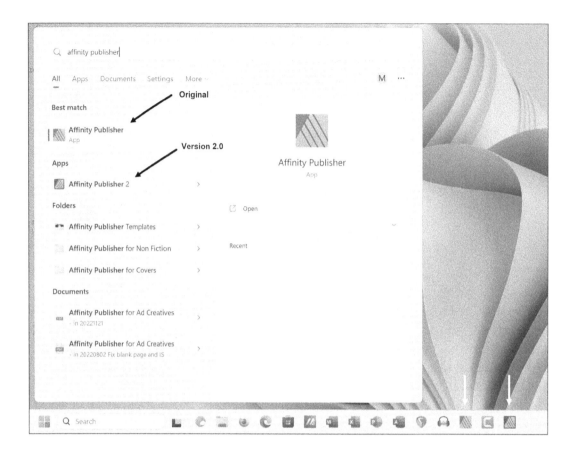

They also have slightly different thumbnails. If you look at the bottom right of the screenshot, you can see how the thumbnail for 2.0 (on the right) has a darker appearance to it and a stronger border around the edge.

You'll also be able to tell which version of Affinity you're working in when you open the program because they changed the appearance of the icons.

Here is the left-hand side of the main workspace of both the original Affinity Publisher (which I've labeled 1.0 on the left) and Affinity Publisher 2.0 (on the right):

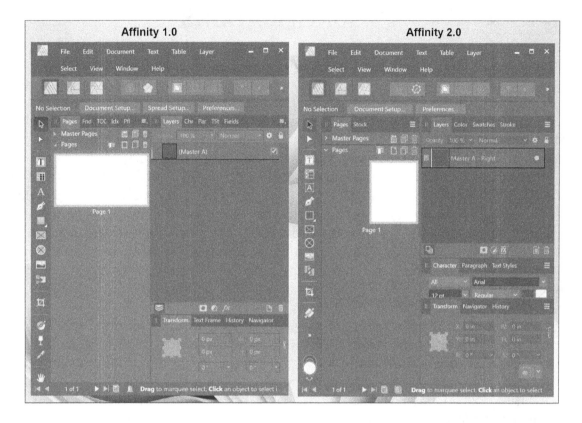

For example, one of the tools we will use is the Frame Text Tool which is that icon at the top of the left column that has a T in it. You can see that in the original Affinity Publisher the T used for the icon was written in a serifed font, but the Affinity Publisher 2.0 version uses a non-serifed font.

IS THIS THE RIGHT BOOK FOR YOU?

This book will walk you through how to use Affinity Publisher 2.0. If you have 1.0 instead, which is possible if you bought Publisher prior to late 2022, then the book you want is *Affinity Publisher for Fiction Layouts*.

You could still use this book, but keep in mind that things may be in different locations or look a little different. Concepts will be the same regardless, how and where will not.

If you are trying to translate between this book and the original version of Affinity Publisher, it may help to check out the videos I've posted on my YouTube channel which walk through various tasks in Affinity that are referenced here.

MY QUALIFICATIONS

Okay. Getting back to using Affinity Publisher for print layouts.

My background is in self-publishing, meaning that I write and then format and publish my own books. At this point between hard cover, regular print, large print editions, and collections, I've published well over two hundred print titles both in fiction and non-fiction. Some of my non-fiction is very image-heavy. For example, I have a few books with almost 200 images in them.

When I first started, I did all of this using Microsoft Word, which is a viable option. My most popular book to-date is still formatted in Word. (Breaks and styles are the key if you're going to use Word, but image resolution can be an issue.)

Later I used tools like Vellum, which really streamlined the process, especially for fiction titles. With Vellum you can take an ebook you've created in that program and have a print book with the click of a button. Other options out there include Draft2Digital's platform and I also believe Atticus although my experience with those is limited.

But for me I needed more control, especially on the non-fiction side. That's how I found my way to Affinity Publisher, which is similar to Adobe InDesign but doesn't require a subscription fee. (At least as of now it is still a one-time purchase.)

At this point I have formatted probably over a hundred titles in Affinity Publisher and am very pleased with it. I will note here that most of those were done in the original Affinity Publisher so I am writing this book from the perspective of "I know how to do it in the original version, where is it in 2.0?"

Now, to be clear: I do not have a professional publication background, so it is possible I will use different terminology than the pros or that I may do things in my own, weird, quirky way that works for me but isn't the "best" way to do it. My approach to learning things is to dive in and get it working well enough that I can get on to the next thing, so I am not promising you that I know every single way to do everything in Affinity Publisher. I'm just promising you that this way works, isn't time consuming, and will give you a nice finished product.

HOW THIS IS GOING TO WORK

The rest of this book is going to walk you through how to create a basic print title from start to finish, including how to set up master pages, flow your text, and create and apply text styles. We'll also cover how to export your final product. The print title we're going to create will use a small accent image so that you can see how to incorporate that with your text.

I'll then show you a few tricks so that you don't have to do this level of work ever again. (Once you have your first print layout created, it's pretty easy to use it again and more than halve the required time to create your next title.)

ADDITIONAL RESOURCES

Affinity has excellent help resources. I highly recommend looking at the videos available on their website under the Learn tab up top if you ever get stuck. Here is the link for Publisher on Desktop: https://affinity.serif.com/en-us/learn/publisher/desktop/

(This is how I initially learned the program, but for me the videos weren't in an intuitive order, so I only realized that they covered everything I needed about two thirds of the way through watching them. Hence the reason I wrote the first version of this book.)

They also have an excellent support community and user forums. I usually find relevant discussions via a web search for Affinity Publisher and whatever it is I need to know more about. So, "Affinity Publisher flow text", for example.

Keep in mind, though, that they are updating the product on a regular basis and that 1.0 versus 2.0 are different, so if you find an old answer it may no longer be applicable. Something that you couldn't do before may now be possible or where an option is located may have changed.

They do also have an Affinity Help website that you can access in the top menu of Affinity Publisher under Help or by searching on the internet for Affinity Publisher Help. It's best to access it through the program to make sure you access the version that corresponds to Affinity 2.0.

You can search there as well, although for me personally that is usually my last stop. You need to know the proper terms to find what you want and then sometimes the explanations assume a graphic design level of knowledge that I, at least, don't have.

ASSUMPTIONS

I am going to assume some basic knowledge of how programs like this one would work. Meaning I'm not going to define for you here terms like dialogue box, dropdown menu, control shortcut (Ctrl + C), etc. I do define those terms in my beginner Word books and they may actually be visible in preview if you need that. And you'll have screenshots here, too. But if you aren't at least that familiar with working in software programs, this may be a big stretch for you.

You should be comfortable working in a word processing program like Word before you try to tackle Affinity Publisher. (In my opinion. Try if you want, but it will be harder for you.)

I'm also going to assume that you have basic familiarity with how print books are formatted. I may define things like front matter, back matter, or discuss where to start chapters in passing, but it is not going to be the focus of this book.

Okay, then. Let's get started and open Affinity Publisher.

GETTING STARTED

I'm going to assume that you've already purchased and downloaded Affinity Publisher. If not, you can do that at https://affinity.serif.com/en-us/ or the equivalent site in your country. (I believe that en-us is the part that says United States and in English.)

Go ahead and open it now. The version I'm working in is 2.0.4. This is what it looks like for me when I open it:

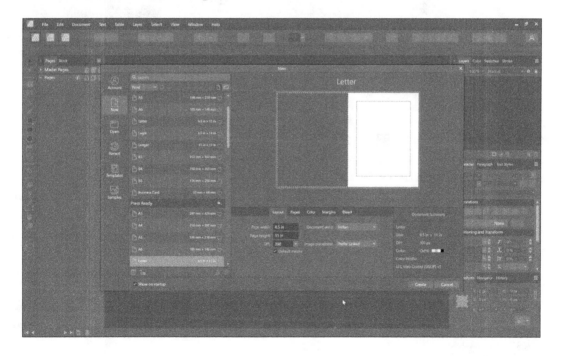

It has a New dialogue box visible in the center of the screen with the main workspace visible behind that, although they are the same color so do blend a bit.

To work on a project in Affinity Publisher you need to create a document. You can either choose one using the New dialogue box or, if that's closed, use the File menu up top, which is usually what I use to reopen a recent file.

But for now we don't need to create a document because I want to set up your workspace first. So click on the X in the top right corner of the New dialogue box to close it. You should now see the default workspace that Affinity gives you:

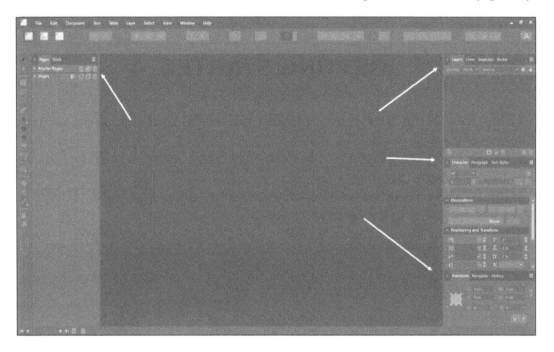

On both sides of the workspace there are panels docked by default. These are essentially task panes that give you options related to specific functions you might want to perform.

For example, the Pages panel, in the top left, shows your master pages as well as any pages that you've added to create your document. The Layers panel, in the top right, shows the layers on a given page—all of your images or text frames in our case.

The panels you see by default in Affinity Publisher are just a dozen or so of the panels that are actually available to you. If you want to see all of the available panels, go to the Window option at the top of the screen. Most of the dropdown menu you'll see below that are panels that you can choose to display in your workspace.

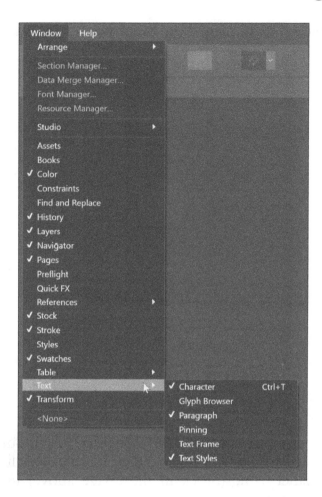

The list starts with Assets and goes down to Transform. References, Table, and Text all have secondary dropdown menus that show more panel choices. In the screenshot above you can see the Text secondary dropdown menu.

(Note that this is different from the original Affinity Publisher where they were under View in the top menu and the panels were all listed under a Studio secondary menu.)

If a panel is already visible, it shows a white check mark to the left of the name. You can see that with Color, History, and Layers, for example.

To close a panel that's open that you don't want, click on its name in the dropdown.

You can also close a panel from the main workspace by left-clicking and dragging the panel from its name tab so that the panel is no longer docked. Once you have it isolated, click on the X in the top right corner of the panel.

Here I have left-clicked and dragged the Stock panel so that it is standalone:

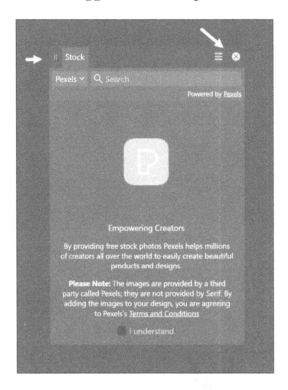

I can now click on that X in the top right corner to close it out.

If I instead wanted to reposition the panel, I could left-click and drag using the tab with the panel name (Stock in the image above) until the panel was positioned where I wanted it.

To dock a panel in a new location, you just drag it to a new dockable location, which we'll cover in a moment. Right now what we are going to do is build the workspace I want you to use for the rest of this book.

The first step is to remove the panels we don't need. That includes Stock on the top left side and Stroke on the top right side. I clicked and dragged them out and then used the X to close them rather than try to find them in the dropdown menu, but either way works.

Next, we need to move a few panels around.

On the top right side I prefer to have Layers, Character, Paragraph, Text Styles, and then Fields. I have nothing in the middle section. And then in the bottom right I put Transform, Text Frame, Swatches, and Color, but usually the only one down there I use for book layouts is Transform. You can also leave Navigator and History there if you want.

So we need to left-click on Character, Paragraph, and Text Styles and then drag to move each one up to the top right. We'll start with Character.

Left-click on the tab with the name and hold that left-click as you drag the panel into its new location. You should see the area flash blue first, but keep going until you see the tab next to any existing tabs. Like here where Character is now next to Layers and Color:

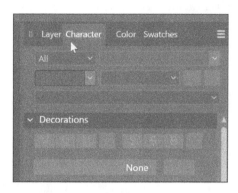

Release your left-click and that panel should now be one of the options in that row. (If you release the left-click when it flashes blue, that panel will be placed in its own row and not docked next to the other panel choices.)

Move the other two panels (Paragraph and Text Styles) into place using the same technique.

The reason I don't have a middle set of panels is because I like to be able to see my full list of layers and text styles without them cutting off because there's a panel below them. You'll see more of that in action later.

Next we need to add a few new panels that aren't available by default. Those are Find and Replace, Table of Contents, Index, and Preflight on the top left and Fields on the top right.

First, click on Pages, go to the Window option up top and then find each of those panels I listed for the top left.

Find and Replace is in the main menu and should insert right next to Pages. If it doesn't, drag the standalone panel into place so that it docks next to Pages. Repeat this with Table of Contents, Index, and Preflight. Table of Contents and Index are under the References secondary dropdown menu. Preflight is in the main dropdown.

For a basic title like we're going to create in this book, you won't use Table of Contents or Index, but this is my overall print set-up so I'm having you add them now. You don't have to if you don't want to. Index is for non-fiction.

Now click on the tab for Text Styles in the top right corner and then add

Fields which is in the References secondary dropdown menu.

For me, that one came in as an undocked panel, so I had to left-click and drag until it docked next to Text Styles.

For each section that contains panels, you will have only one panel visible at a time. So I can see only one of the Pages, Find and Replace, Table of Contents, Index, or Preflight panels at a time. Same with Layers, Character, Paragraph, Text Styles, or Fields. And with Transform, Swatches, Color, Navigator, and History.

My default is to have Pages, Layers, and Transform available and then to only click to the other panels as needed when working on a print layout.

Here is my final layout:

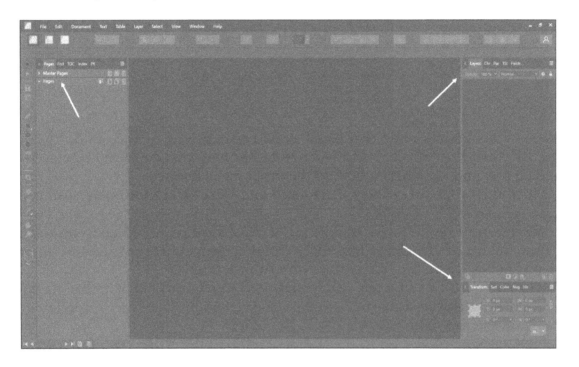

Since I also use Affinity Publisher to design covers and advertising images and I use very different panels when working on images, I like to save this layout so I can flip back and forth between my book layout workspace and my image workspace.

To do that you create a Studio Preset. This is also done under the Window option. Go to Window and then Studio, and choose Add Preset.

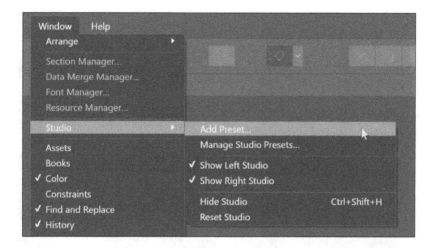

Click on that option to bring up the Add Preset dialogue box and type in the name you want to use:

Click OK to add that workspace layout (which they refer to as a studio) as a Studio Preset.

Affinity Publisher should default to the last layout you were using when you closed the program. To change to a different workspace layout, go to Window and then Studio and then choose the preset from the secondary dropdown menu:

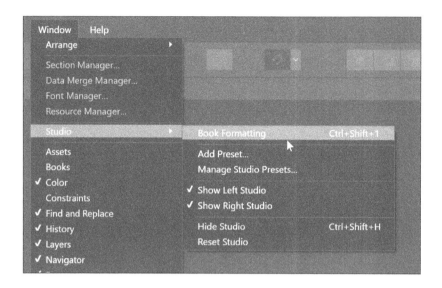

Presets also will have a Ctrl shortcut assigned by default. The first one you create will be Ctrl + Shift + 1, the next one will be Ctrl + Shift + 2, etc.

If you ever decide that you need to rename a preset, you can do so by choosing Manage Studio Presets from that secondary dropdown menu. Click on the preset you want to rename and then the Rename option. This is also where you can go to delete an existing preset.

To change a preset, create your new workspace layout and then choose Add Preset, but give the preset the exact same name of your existing preset. Affinity will show a dialogue box that asks if you want to replace the existing studio preset. Say Yes and it will overwrite your former layout with the new one.

NEW FILE TEMPLATE

Okay. Now that we have our workspace set up, it's time to tell Affinity the type of document you want to create.

This is not going to be the same for every single person creating a print book. For example, my non-fiction computer books are 7.5 x 9.25 inches. My large print titles are 6 x 9 inches. And my regular paperbacks are 5.25 x 8 inches.

So you need to know starting off what size book you want to create. My advice is to look at books published by traditional publishers in your genre or subject area. You can usually see the book measurements listed on the book page on Amazon.

Also, make sure that you are looking at the right version of that book. For self-publishing most books are published in a trade format paperback size, which is the larger paperback. Don't look at the mass market paperback size.

If you're going to publish through Amazon's KDP program, be sure to choose a print size that is one of their listed sizes. You can find this by searching for Print Options under the Help function at their website. If you're going to do a hardcover version through them (only case-laminate style is available at this point in time), note that there is a much more limited selection of sizes available to you.

One thing to keep in mind with most print titles is that they use what's called mirrored margins. This means that the inner margins of two facing pages are the same size and the outer margins are the same size.

The inner margin is usually going to be bigger than the outer margin because there needs to be space for the pages to be bound into a book.

If you need to know what margins to use on a book and aren't sure, I'd recommend starting with the print templates provided by Amazon.

Okay. Once you've decided what size book you're going to create, you need to start that document in Affinity. Since we're already in the program, we can go to File and then choose New to bring up the New dialogue box. (Which I will note looks very different in Affinity Publisher 2.0 compared to the original program.)

Here it is:

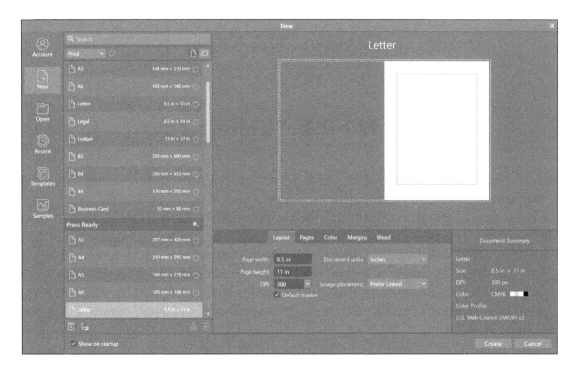

You can see on the left-hand side that Affinity provides a number of pre-formatted options such as Letter, Legal, Business Card, and A4. These are listed under categories such as Print and Press Ready.

Scroll down and you'll see other categories listed, including Photo, Web, Devices, and Architectural. You can also create your own categories.

The dropdown menu at the very top will let you jump to a specific category or you can use the scroll bar on the right-hand side.

Each document listing also shows the basic dimensions for that document on the right-hand side of the listing. 148 mm x 210 mm for A5, for example.

Note at the bottom below the document listing you can also check or uncheck a box, "Show On Startup", to show this New dialogue box when you open Affinity Publisher.

The right-hand side of the dialogue box displays a sample two-page spread for the selected document, including any margins and bleed that have been set.

Below that are tabs for Layout, Pages, Color, Margins, and Bleed where you can specify those settings for that document.

Here we have an 8.5 x 11 inch document that is just a single page with the Layout tab selected.

None of the default documents are ever what I want. Which means I have to create my own. Since we're talking about print, I recommend starting with a template that is either set up for inches or set up for millimeters. You could technically start with any of the existing ones and then change the document units in the Layout tab, but the one time I tried that it did not go well. So I don't try to do that anymore.

Instead, I find a template that already has the correct units selected. In this case, I am going to start with the 8.5 x 11 inch option and then I'm going to change the dimensions in the Layout tab.

I want to change the width to 5.25 and the height to 8. Here we are:

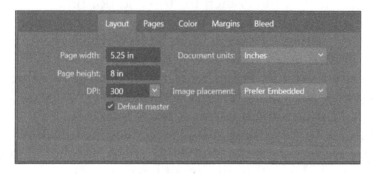

For any book that has images in it, you will need a DPI of 300 or more. I usually set it to 305 to be safe. Also, you need to make a decision to either link to images wherever they're stored or to embed them.

If you embed images, that means that you'll potentially have a very large file size. But it also means that you never run into a situation where Affinity doesn't have the image to use in your document. It will warn you if that happens, but then you'll have to go find that image wherever it is and hope you have it. So for this book where we're just going to have one accent image, I'm going to choose to embed images. If this was non-fiction where I have a hundred-plus images in the book, I'd link my images instead.

Also, you can change this option later if needed. And Affinity will actually suggest that you do so if you work with too many embedded images.

Next, click over to the Pages tab. It should be facing pages, horizontally, start on right, and can have 1 page to start, which means we don't need to change anything here.

After that, click to the Color tab. For most basic print projects, you will want to have a black and white document. (Color is much more expensive to print.)

I use Gray/8 and Greyscale D50. If you are going to use color, then the choice you want here is CMYK not RGB. RGB is for colors on a screen not printed colors. If you're not sure what to use, check with your printer.

The next tab, Margins, is key. As I mentioned above, you can pull your margins from the KDP templates that Amazon offers. They are provided in Microsoft Word and you can go to Page Layout, Margins to see what values Amazon recommends. Combine the inside margin and gutter values to get your inside margin measurement if you do so.

For me for a 5.25 x 8 book, I use an inner margin of .9 inch, an outer margin of .6 inch, and then top and bottom margins of .76 inches which is what I pulled from an old Amazon template.

For large print I use 6 x 9 and my margins are 1 inch for the inner margin, .75 inch for the outer margin, and .9 inch for top and bottom.

I don't think you need bleed for a basic print book, but mine have it because I never changed it, so mine all have .125 inch bleed which seems to be the default value they use. (When you export it will normally export to PDF without the bleed. If you ever use Affinity Publisher to create a cover for your Amazon KDP print book then you will need to export with bleed.)

Okay, that's it. Our document layout is ready to go.

If you don't care to save these settings you can just click on Create. If you think you may want to use these settings to create another document at some point then you should make this document into a preset.

What I usually do is open the last book I formatted, delete out the contents, and then put in the new contents for my new title, so I don't need a preset for my print books, I just click on Create.

But let's walk through how to turn this into a preset, just in case.

At the top of the preview section of the New dialogue box, you'll see the title of the preset you're working with. If it's been edited, there will be a star next to the name, and you'll also be able to see a little box with a plus sign and also an update icon:

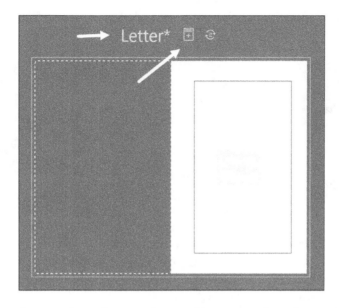

If you click on the update icon, that will overwrite the existing document template to reflect the changes you made.

If you click on the box with the plus sign, that will open the Create Preset dialogue box allowing you to keep the original template as-is but also create a new preset based upon your changes:

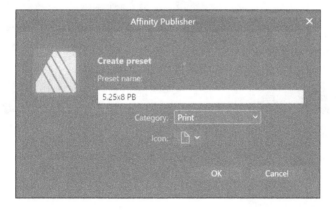

Type in the name you want, choose the category and icon, and then click on OK.

If you are not coming to Affinity Publisher 2.0 from the original Affinity Publisher and so didn't transfer over existing presets, then your category options will be limited to the default options of Print, Press Ready, etc.

To create a custom category, you can go to the very bottom of the preset listing on the left-hand side and click on the icon for Create Category. See here where the arrow is pointing at the option and then the Create Category dialogue box is shown:

If you create the category after you already created your preset, simply left-click on the preset and drag it down to the new category you created.

Once that preset is saved, make sure you have it selected, and click on Create to create your document. Affinity will then display that document in your workspace.

In our case what you're going to see is a single page of a document since we chose 1 for the number of pages for our default document:

The white space is the document page. The blue border within that white space shows where our specified margins are. The blue border outside the white space shows where the bleed border is.

The document is not actually formatted for text right now, it's just a blank slate, which you can see in the Pages panel which shows a blank page. (The Pages section of the Pages panel will always show how the document page would actually look if printed.) Those blue lines are just guidelines to follow when placing your elements.

Our next step is to create what are called Master Pages, which let us take this base and add elements like headers, footers, images, and text frames that remain constant across pages of that type.

Let's do that now. Don't worry, it will make more sense as we work through it.

MASTER PAGES

In my opinion, master pages are the core of what makes using Affinity Publisher so much better than using Word for print formatting.

Master pages are basically templates that you create that include your page numbering, your headers, your footers, any images you want on that type of page, and your text placement.

I create a master page for every type of two-page spread I need in a book, but you could also create one-page master pages, that's really up to you. Either way works. One-page master pages probably mean less chance of an error, but I find two-page master pages more intuitive to work with.

For a basic book like we're creating here, applying master pages is probably 75% of the formatting work. Text styles are the other big chunk of it.

We're going to create a total of nine master pages:

1. Title

2. Also By

3. Copyright and Chapter Start

4. No Text and Chapter Start

5. Text and Chapter Start

6. Text and Text

7. Chapter Start and Text

8. Text and About the Author

9. No Text and About the Author

Depending on where your text falls and the formatting choices you make, you may not need all of those. Or you may want to change them up. For example, you may prefer a Copyright and Also By page instead of a Copyright and Chapter Start page. But by the time we've built those nine master pages you should have the ability to create any master page you need.

If you were doing single-page master pages, then what you'd do is:

1. Title

2. Also By

3. Copyright

4. Chapter Start

5. Text

6. No Text

7. About the Author

We'll circle back to this when we create each of these, but if you're doing single-page master pages, be sure to use an alignment choice for your headers and footers that works on both left-hand and right-hand pages. Namely, you'll want to center your text or choose to align away from or towards the spine. (Usually not towards the spine, but it is an option.)

Okay. We're going to just dive in in a minute and create a few of these and it will start to make more sense, but first I want to work through a few high-level things related to master pages. (I'm assuming from this point forward that your workspace looks like mine. If it doesn't, adjust as needed.)

Go to the top left corner of your workspace where we placed the Pages panel and click on it.

You should see two sections, one for Master Pages and one for Pages. Click on Master Pages to expand that section. The panel should look like this once you do:

OPEN MASTER PAGE

Double-click on that Master A thumbnail in the Master Pages section to bring it up in the main workspace. Note that the master page has a left-hand and a right-hand page to it by default.

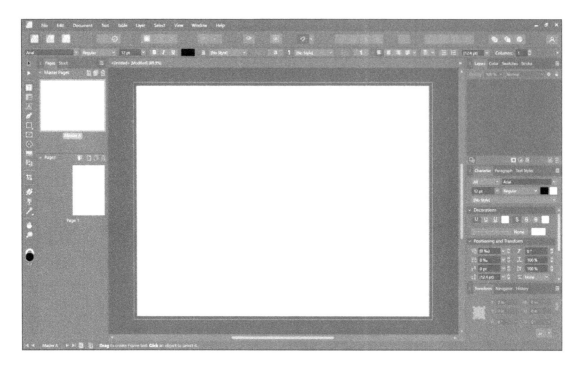

Whatever page or master page is in your main workspace is the one that can be edited at that point in time and the one that will show in the other panels.

RENAME MASTER PAGE

To rename a master page, click on the name under or next to its thumbnail in the Master Pages section of the Pages panel. A white box will appear around the name and the name will be highlighted in blue. Type in the new name you want and hit Enter.

ADD NEW MASTER PAGE

To add a new master page, right-click on an existing master page and choose Insert Master. This will bring up an Insert Master dialogue box where you can specify the name for the master page and any difference in dimensions or margins.

We will not change any of those settings in this book, so just type in the new master page name. If you do want to do one-page master pages instead of two-page master pages, click on Single instead of Facing in this dialogue box before creating the master page.

Another option is to right-click on a master page thumbnail and choose to Duplicate it. That will not only copy the page settings but any layers that have been placed onto that master page.

We will use the Duplicate option when creating our interior master pages to save time.

Be careful when you duplicate a master page, because by default Affinity will keep the first master page in the workspace. Which means you can end up making edits to the "wrong" master page. Always double-click on the thumbnail for the master page spread you want to edit just to be safe before you start making your edits to avoid this issue.

SEE MORE MASTER PAGES IN THE PAGES PANEL

If you're mostly working with master pages and you want to see more than just one at a time in the Pages panel, you can click on the Pages header in the panel to minimize the Pages section.

Here it is before I do that with both Master Pages and Pages expanded:

Here it is when I've minimized Pages and have the Master Pages section fully visible:

REARRANGE MASTER PAGES

To rearrange the order of your master pages in the Master Pages section, left-click and drag the thumbnail of the master page you want to move. Make sure that both pages are selected when moving a two-page master page and be sure to drag to the side of the other master page where you want to move it. You should see a blue line where it will move to.

I usually try to keep mine in order from start of the book to end of the book. So I'll have the Title master page at the top and the About the Author master page at the end. But you could do it alphabetically if that works better for you.

CHANGE THUMBNAIL SIZE IN PAGES PANEL

To change the size of the thumbnails in the Pages panel, left-click on the three lines at the end of the row with the panel tabs while you have the Pages panel selected:

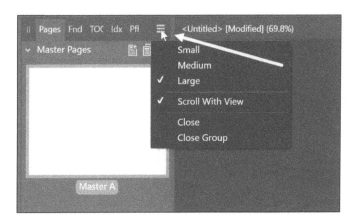

Choose the thumbnail size you want. Small thumbnails will put the master page name to the side instead of below the thumbnail.

I prefer to use large thumbnails because it's easier to see the difference in the elements on each master page at a glance with a larger image.

DELETE A MASTER PAGE

To delete a master page, right-click on the thumbnail for the master page and choose Delete from the dropdown menu.

* * *

Okay. That's the basics of how to work with the Master Pages section of the Pages panel. Now let's go create our first master page, the Title Page.

TITLE MASTER PAGE

The Title page is going to be the first page in your document and will simply show the title and author for the book. Here is what the master page is going to look like when we're done:

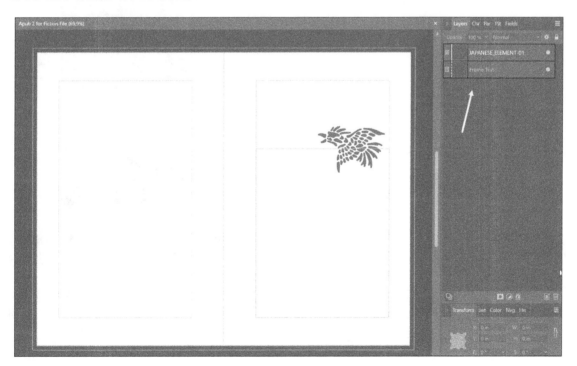

It has two elements, the text frame where we can enter the book title and the accent image. For each master page you want to include the elements that will *always* appear on that page, which is why this master page does not include any text.

Also, remember that I'm doing a very simple layout here. You can obviously take what we do and fancy it up as much as you want later. This is one way of doing things, not the only way.

To get started, go to the Master Pages section of the Pages panel and rename the first thumbnail Title Page.

(For a new document there should only be the one thumbnail, but if you added master pages in the last chapter and didn't later delete them you may have more than one.)

Next, double-click on that thumbnail. Your workspace should look something like this:

As I mentioned before, those blue borders do not appear in the final printed document. They are just there to let you know where to place the various elements.

They also do not constrain any text or images that you add. So if you typed text directly onto this page, it would go right across those blue lines without a problem.

To constrain text to a specific area, you need to use a text frame. So let's do that now.

Our text is going to go on the right-hand page and needs to fall somewhere within the blue rectangle visible on the white space on that page. I don't want the text to start that high though, so I'm going to place a text frame that is the same width as the blue rectangle but not as tall.

To add a text frame we use the Frame Text Tool which is on the left-hand side at the top of the list of tools. It looks like a T in a square and you can see its name if you hold your mouse over it like I've done here:

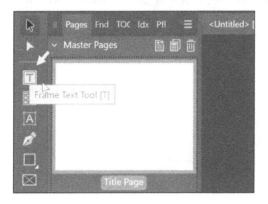

Click on that icon and then left-click and drag in the main workspace to create your frame. As you left-click and drag you'll see a blue frame appear in the workspace, like this:

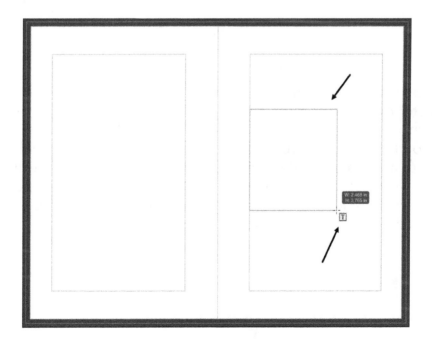

You can see that I'm using the Frame Text Tool because my cursor is that T in a box and you can see the outline of the frame that I'm creating there in the middle of the right-hand page.

I want this frame to line up with the edges of the available space we set for our text in the document setup stage, so I am going to keep dragging the edges of that text frame until it aligns with both sides and the bottom of that original blue rectangle.

But let's say I stopped too soon so I just have this text frame that is too small for what I want.

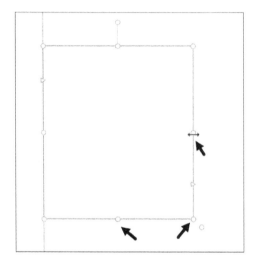

I can click on the text frame and then left-click on any of the white circles around the perimeter or in the corners and hold that left-click as I drag to resize the frame to what I need.

When you reach the blue rectangle with your text frame, you will see either a green or red line appear. If the frame is aligned with the lines on the sides, the line you see will be green. If it's aligned on the top or bottom, the line will be red.

You can see both here as well as a green line through the center that indicates the text frame is centered left-to-right to that blue rectangle:

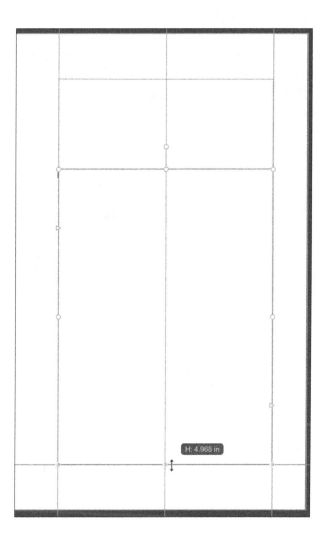

The alignment lines also extend off of the page. This is probably a little hard to see in the black and white print version because you won't see the colors of the lines, but you can still see a horizontal line there at the bottom that extends off the page to both sides as well as three vertical lines that extend off the top and bottom of the page.

When you see the green and red lines that means that your text frame border is aligned with the blue rectangle that outlines where your text can go.

These alignment lines will actually appear for all elements on a page as we'll see later, so for a more complex layout you'd need to be a little more careful that it's aligned to the correct element, but for now this works just fine.

If you're not seeing those red and green lines, that's because they only appear when Snapping is enabled.

It looks like it is the default in Affinity Publisher 2.0 for Snapping to be enabled, but if it isn't for you, then go to the middle of the options menu up top and find the image that looks like a horseshoe-shaped magnet. (If you hold your mouse over it, it will say Snapping.)

Click on the dropdown arrow next to the image and make sure that the Enable Snapping box at the top left is checked:

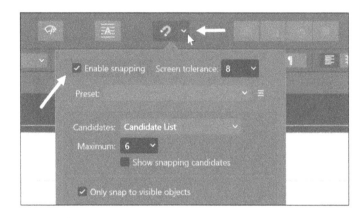

Snapping is something that I leave on at all times because it is often the easiest way to align the various elements in your document. If, however, you find it annoying you can also go there to uncheck that box and turn it off as needed.

Okay. So insert your text frame, keeping in mind that the top of the *text frame* is where your title text will start. Here's mine:

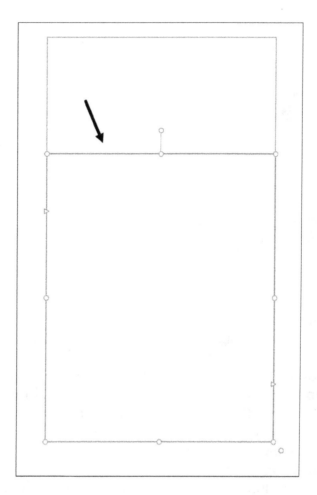

I've clicked on the text frame so you can see its outline by looking at the little circles around the perimeter. It overlaps with the blue rectangle from our document setup on three sides, but is not as tall as that rectangle.

Now let's add an image. (You can skip ahead if you don't want to use one, but I want to show you how this works.)

I find that simple images that use solid colors work best for something like this, because they easily translate to black and white. Here, I have a number that I can choose from courtesy of Design Cuts packages I've bought over the years (https://www.designcuts.com/):

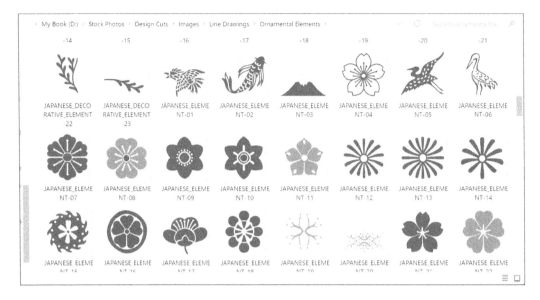

Any of these could probably work, the question would be where to position them relative to the text to make it look "good". No guarantee I'm going to pull that off here, but I will at least show you the how of it.

Be sure if you do use an image in your book design that you have the rights to do so. The Design Cuts packages come with commercial rights. Depositphotos and Shutterstock are two other places I've bought images in the past.

(Also, you want the image you use to be a high enough resolution so that it prints at 300 DPI or more when printed in its final size. That shouldn't be an issue if you buy the image from a professional site, but could be if you try to use a personal photo or an image you saved from a website since most websites or images viewed on a computer look fine at a lower resolution.)

We're going to place this image directly onto the document. (The other option would be to use a picture frame, which is covered in the next book in this series.)

To place the image, first click on the black arrow on the top left of the workspace. This is the Move Tool and it will get you away from using the Frame Text Tool.

Next, click on the Place Image Tool option on the left-hand side, which looks like a drawing of mountains:

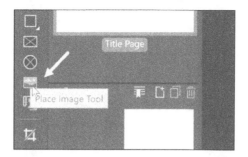

That is going to bring up the Open dialogue box. Navigate to where you have your picture saved, select it, and then choose Open.

Your cursor will now look like a fat white arrow with another arrow pointing down at a bluish-colored oval:

Move the cursor to where you want to place the image and left-click and drag until the image is the size you want. When you let up on the left-click you will have your image in your document surrounded by a border.

Don't worry too much about getting the placement or size exactly right, just get it close to where you want it initially.

If you already clicked on the Move Tool before you started, you can then left-click anywhere on the image and drag it into position.

Here I have placed the image so that the right edge is aligned to the right edge of the text frame and the center of the image is aligned to the top of the text frame:

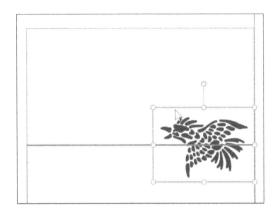

In the ebook and color versions of this book you'll see that those lines are green and red to show the alignment. In the black and white version they should be darker.

If you don't like the size of the image, you can either left-click and drag from the corner of the image to change its size, or you can change the image dimensions in the Transform panel by adjusting the W or H (width or height) values.

Remember that we placed the Transform panel in the bottom right corner.

If you use the Transform panel to change an image, be sure to lock the aspect ratio so that both the width and height will change at the same time so that the image stays proportionate.

You do this by clicking on the little "lock" image to the right of the width and height values before you change either one. Hold your mouse over it and you'll see that it's the Lock Aspect Ratio option:

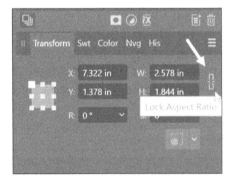

If you somehow change an image so that it is not in the proportions it was when you imported it, Affinity will warn you about this in the Preflight panel. You can see here that I stretched this image sideways without also adjusting its height:

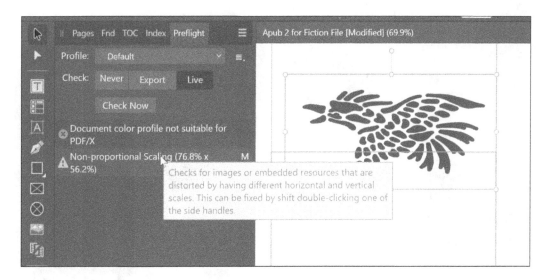

The second noted item in the Preflight panel is telling me that. I've placed my mouse over the warning so you can also see what it means and how Affinity tells you to fix it.

To fix it, hold down the Shift key and then double-click on one of the circles on the side of the image to get the image back to proportional scaling. Be careful, though, because that might make the image a size you don't want to use and you'll then have to resize again. But it does at least fix the image proportions quickly.

Okay. So. Import your image and then position it where you want it relative to your text frame and the margins of your document.

I prefer not to let my images overflow into the margins. You can, though, it's not forbidden. But if you allow the image to go all the way to the edge of the page, I believe you then need to choose a different bleed option when you publish and would need to extend it past the white space to where the bleed border is.

Here is our final Title Page master page with the Pages and Layers panels visible:

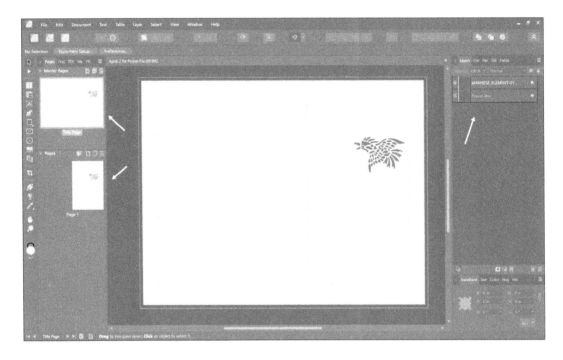

You can see in the Master Pages section of the Pages panel which elements of the document will actually display when this page is exported. Namely, just the image we inserted. The text frame will not be visible nor are the outlines that show where the margins are.

In the Pages section, you can see that because this is the first page of our document and it starts on the right-hand side that only the right-hand side of this master page will show in the final document.

Also, if you look to the Layers panel, which was visible in the screenshot at the start of this chapter, you will see that we have added two elements to this master page. One is the image and one is the text frame.

Now let's go down to the Pages section of the Pages panel and bring up our actual document so we can add our book title and see how that works because we have one more tweak to make here to finalize this master page.

ADD TITLE PAGE TO DOCUMENT

By default, because we only have the one master page, Affinity will use that master page for the document that's shown in the Pages section of the Pages panel which is only one page long at this point.

To open and edit that page, go to the Pages section of the Pages panel and double-click on its thumbnail. This will bring up the page in the main workspace.

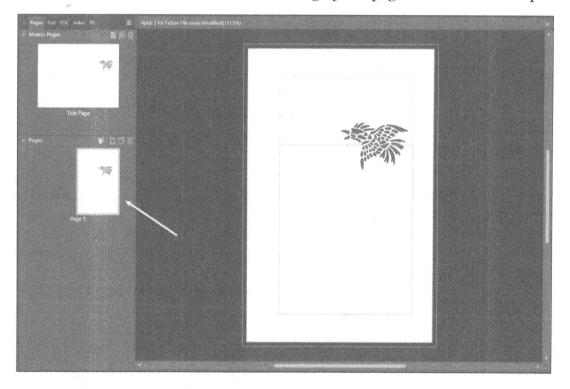

This is where you want to add your title text. Not in the Master Pages section, but in the Pages section.

To do that, click on the Artistic Text Tool which is an A in a box, two below the Frame Text Tool:

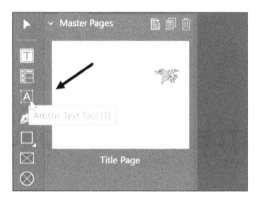

Next, click into the text frame in your document and start typing:

Here I have typed "The Best Book Since Sliced Bread" and you can see that the text appears at the top of that text frame.

I don't like the font or font size, though. And we also need to deal with the issue of the text disappearing behind the image. Let's deal with the font first.

Use Ctrl + A to select all of the text you just typed. It should highlight that text in blue. You could also select the text using a left-click and drag or using Shift and the arrow keys.

Next, go to the dynamic menu up top (it changes depending on which tool is currently in use). There should be three dropdowns there as well as buttons to select for bold, italics, and underline:

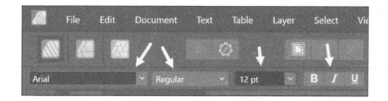

The first dropdown is for font. It lets you choose a font to use:

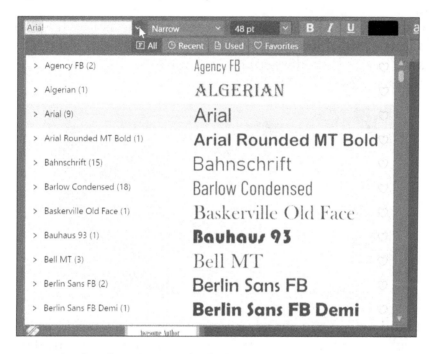

If you have a particular font in mind, click into the field that displays the current font name and start typing the font name you want. The dropdown menu will shift to that part of the listing and you can then click on the font name.

If you're not sure, you can see what each font looks like because each entry is written in that font. Note the difference between Algerian, Arial, Bahnschrift, and Bauhaus 93 in this list, for example. Also, as you put your mouse over each of the fonts in the list the selected text in your document will temporarily change to show how that font will look when applied to that text.

Which fonts are available is going to depend on you and which fonts you have loaded onto your computer. Thanks to Design Cuts I have a lot of fonts that I can use. If you haven't purchased fonts, be careful with licensing issues. It's possible you have a font on your computer for "personal" use with Microsoft programs but really shouldn't be using it for commercial design projects. I believe you're safe for the interior of a book but not the cover, but I am not a lawyer so you'll want to research that more thoroughly (or just buy the font you're going to use so it's not an issue).

You can click on the heart icon next to a font to favorite the font. If you do that, then the Favorites tab at the top of the font listing will include it.

You can also click on the Recent or Used tabs at the top of the font listing to see the fonts you've used recently or that have been used in the document at some point.

The next dropdown menu shows the various options you have for that font. It will include any available weights (light, regular, medium, bold, etc.), any italic versions, as well as expanded or condensed versions.

Here you can see that for Arial:

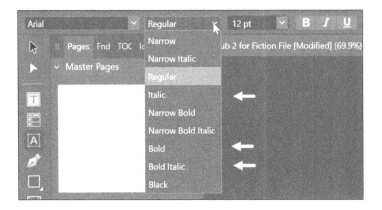

It turns out (and maybe you already know this), but the "bold" version of a font and the "italic" version of a font and the "bold italic" version of a font are all separate files, so you're only going to have those options for a font if you have those specific files loaded on your computer.

In this case, I have regular, (regular) italic, (regular) bold, (regular) bold italic, and also narrow versions of each.

Because I have those options available for the Regular weight that I have selected in the dropdown above, the Bold and Italic buttons are also available for me to click on. (That's the B and the slanted I visible at the end of that same row in the screenshot.)

But for other fonts, like Jupiter here, I don't have all of those options:

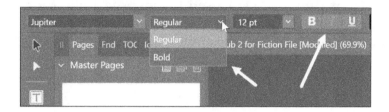

You can see that Jupiter only comes in Regular and Bold. Since there is not an italic version, the slanted I is grayed out.

Finally, the third dropdown there is for the size of your font. The larger the number, the larger the text. You can also type in a value.

If you have text selected, as you place your cursor over a font, font weight, or font size, that text in your document will change to show your selection, but you need to click on the option to apply it.

These same options are also available at the top of the Character panel if you want to use that instead.

I made my changes and here is what I ended up with:

I went with 48 pt Bodoni MT. I used Condensed Italic for the title and just Condensed for the author name.

But you can see that we have a problem. Because the word "book" is running into that image.

We need to tell Affinity to not let that happen. The way you do that is by changing one of the settings for the *image*, which means we need to go back to the master page.

Double-click on the thumbnail for that master page. Go to the Layers panel and click on the layer for the image or click on the image directly in the document.

Once you do that, in the top menu there should be an option for Show Text Wrap Settings (see the screenshot below).

Click on that to bring up the Text Wrap dialogue box:

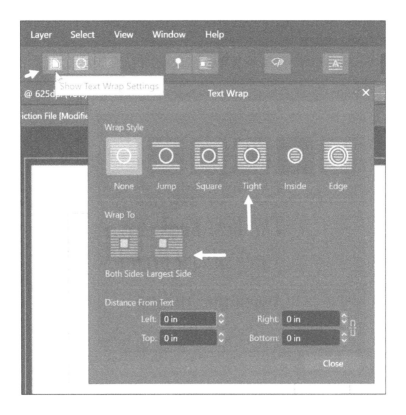

The setting we want to use here is Tight and then Largest Side. This will make sure that any text is kept to the left of our image (the larger side) and that it wraps to the next line as soon as it reaches the point where it would touch the image.

As soon as I made those two selections and closed the dialogue box, the change was reflected on the title page in my document:

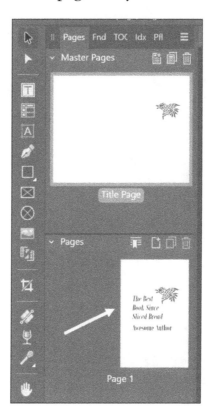

You can see that "book" is now on the second line and that "sliced" also moved to the next line to avoid overlapping with the bird's wing.

That wrap text setting will hold for any other page in the document that uses this master page so it only needs to be set once per master page.

Okay. Next let's do the Also By master page.

ALSO BY MASTER PAGE

The Also By master page is where you can list other titles by that author if there are any. We're going to create one that's very simple and has a text frame on the right-hand page as well as our accent image. It should look like this when it's done:

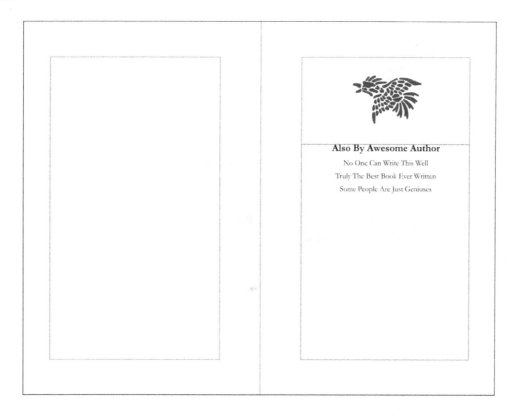

First, we need another master page to work on.

I'm just going to be lazy here and duplicate the Title master page since it already has the two elements we need, a text frame and accent image.

To do that, right-click on the thumbnail for the Title master page and select Duplicate from the dropdown menu.

Scroll down (if needed) to see the new master page. Rename it.

Finally, double-click on that thumbnail to make sure the master page in the main workspace is the correct one.

Because I duplicated the title page, I already have a text frame and an image to work with, so all I have to do is resize or reposition them as needed. And because the Also By text should be consistent across all books in the series, I can add the text into the master page. That will save me effort with later books in the series.

I want to experiment a bit to see what works here. First, I'm going to try making the text start closer to the top of the page. To do that, I need to resize the text frame.

First step is to make sure the Move Tool is selected. That's the black arrow at the top of the left-hand set of icons.

Next, I can either go to the Layers panel and click on the Frame Text layer there, or I can click directly on the text frame in my master page. I usually choose to use the Layers panel.

Once I've done that I just left-click and drag from the blue circle at the top of the frame until I've changed the height to what I want.

Okay. So I did that.

Next, I want to make the image smaller, so I click on the image layer. I can then either use the Transform panel (making sure the aspect ratio is locked) or left-click and drag from one of the corners of the image to resize it.

Once I've changed the image size I need text to really see if this works. So I click on the Artistic Text Tool and then click into the text frame and add the titles I want to list. While I'm there I want to make sure the font is the same as I used on the Title master page, Bodoni MT.

Here we go:

I don't like it. Left-aligned was fine for the title page, but I want this text centered. And actually, given the number of titles I think the text starts too high on the page.

If I'm going to bring that text back down, then it makes sense to have the text frame be the same height as the title page. So let's go back to the Title master page real quick and click on the text frame and then look at the Transform panel:

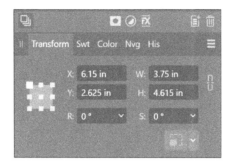

I want my text frame on my Also By master page to use all of these values. X and Y show where on the page the text frame is located, W and H set its size. I don't have to change all four values, though, just H and Y.

So let me do that. I take the H and Y values from the Title master page and apply them to the text frame on the Also By master page. Now I have a text frame that is the exact same height as the prior page.

Another way I could've done this was to delete the text frame on the Also By master page, go to the Title master page, click on the text frame layer, use Ctrl + C to copy it, go back to the Also By master page and click on it, and then use Ctrl + V to paste the text frame I copied.

Often that will put the copied element into the exact same location on the new master page.

Or I could've just undone (Ctrl + Z) my changes on the Also By master page until I was back to the original version which was a copy of the Title master page.

But since I'd already typed in text, using the Transform panel seemed like the easiest option.

Now that I've changed the text frame height, that creates a lot of white space at the top of the page, so I think I'm going to center the image this time. To do that, I just left-click on the image and drag until the image is centered in that white space above the text frame but still within the blue rectangle that shows where text should go.

If you ever center an image in a print layout using the Snapping lines, be sure that you're centering to the blue rectangle that shows where text should be as opposed to the whole page. Remember that we have uneven margins to allow for the fact that the inner margin also needs space for binding the pages, which means that the center of the page will not be the same as the center of the area where your text goes.

Usually Affinity will show both lines if you move the image around. You want the outer center line, not the inner one.

Okay. If we're going to center the image, then we also need to center the text.

(It's currently left-aligned.)

To do that, we can select the text and then use the dynamic menu up top. The text alignment options are towards the right-hand side of that menu:

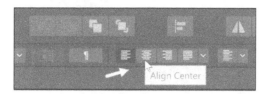

The first option, which is currently selected, is Align Left, next to that is Align Center, followed by Align Right, and then a dropdown of additional options.

Above I have my cursor over the Align Center option so you can see the description. I can just click on that to apply it.

If you don't want to use the dynamic menu, you can also go to the top of the Paragraph panel to find those same alignment options, as well as the ones in the dropdown menu:

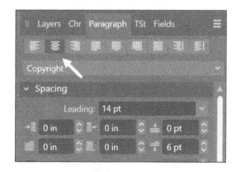

And here we go:

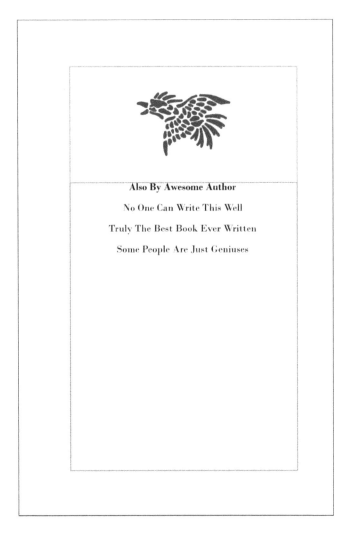

A centered image and centered text with a text frame that matches the title page. That works for me.

* * *

Now let's add the Also By page spread to our document.

First step is to go to the Pages section of the Pages panel, right click on the thumbnail there, and choose Add Pages.

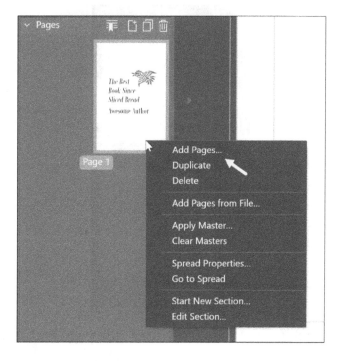

This will open the Add Pages dialogue box. We want to add 2 pages, After the page we just right-clicked on, and we want to change the Master Page dropdown menu to Also By:

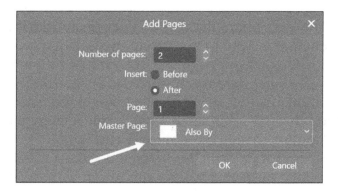

Then we click OK and now in our Pages section, which shows the actual pages of our document, we have our next two pages:

Done. We have a three-page document with a title page and an also by page.

* * *

A quick caution.

If you put text on the master page, like we did here, that's where you should then edit that text.

It can be easy to forget where the text was originally added and to then make changes in the document instead of the master page. But if you do that, then any changes you make to that master page will not carry through to the document.

For example, I just edited the font on the Also By master page. When I hadn't touched the text used on that page in my main document, the font change immediately carried through. But when I had made a change to that text in the main document, the font change did not carry through.

That may sound confusing. You'll understand what I'm talking about if you ever end up making that mistake. I usually run into it with the copyright box that we're about to create.

Basically, if something is on a master page, best practice is to edit it there even if you can edit it in the main document.

COPYRIGHT AND CHAPTER START MASTER PAGE

Those were both very simple master pages that only had two elements. Now we're going to create a slightly more complex master page, the Copyright and Chapter Start master page, which uses text frames on both pages and also includes a footer with the page number:

First step, go to the Master Pages section of the Pages panel and Duplicate the Also By master page. Rename it. Double-click on the thumbnail to be sure that you're on the correct master page.

Next, delete the Also By text but leave the text frame and the image. Also, click into the text frame and change the alignment back to Align Left.

Now we need to look at that text frame on the right-hand page and decide if it needs to be adjusted.

Most chapters in books do not start at the top of the page. It does sometimes happen, but that's the exception more than the rule.

Also, the first time I created a Chapter Start master page in Affinity I created a separate text frame for the chapter title. You could do that, and some of the books in my sample stack on my desk probably did. But it's a lot more effort to do things that way.

Better, in my opinion, when you're just starting out, to set apart your chapter titles using a different font choice, size, and/or alignment. That's what we're going to do here.

Which means that the top of the text frame at the beginning of a Chapter Start page is going to be where the chapter title is shown. The actual text of that chapter will fall somewhere below that.

(You'll see this in action in a bit.)

So the question is, do we think that the text frame as it exists right now is low enough on the page to indicate a chapter start, but also high enough on the page to accommodate a chapter title, and still have the text start at a reasonable point on the page?

For now, I think so. But I may change my mind later when we come up with our chapter title format and drop in the text.

I also think that the placement of the accent image will work for a chapter start, so we can leave that alone as well. (This is why we copied the Also By master page, since those elements were already in a good position for us to reuse.)

Which means all we need to add to this master page is the copyright text and the footer.

Let's do the copyright text first. Click on the Frame Text Tool and then click and drag to place a text frame in the bottom left portion of the text area on the left-hand page. If you have a lot of text that you want to include for your copyright notice, make the text frame tall enough to accommodate it. For me it's usually just a few short lines so I keep my text frame small.

Next, add the copyright text you want to use into the text frame.

I put "Copyright © XXXX Author Name, All Rights Reserved, ISBN: XXXXXX" where those commas are line breaks. I include the XXXX placeholders for the copyright year and ISBN number so I won't forget to update them later:

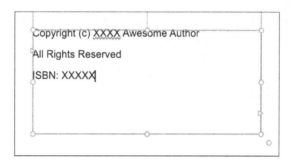

But keep in mind that doing it that way means that you will need to edit this text at some point. I always edit it in the document not in the master page, which means any other changes I make on this master page after I do that won't carry forward to the actual document.

I'm comfortable with that because once I have a template set up I generally don't need to touch my existing master pages, so there are no edits to font, etc. that I need to worry about.

Also, ISBN and copyright year are the very last information I add to a document before finalizing it. That means I should have already caught and fixed any formatting issues with my master pages by that point.

Next step is to use Ctrl + A to select all of that text and change the font and, if wanted, the font size. I always put my copyright notice in the same font I'm going to use for the main body text.

For a regular print book you will want to use some sort of serifed font. Serifed fonts are ones that have little feet at the bottom of letters like "m". I often use Garamond. Times New Roman is another safe choice. If you read a book and really like the font, sometimes they'll have a little paragraph somewhere in the backmatter that tells you what font they used.

For large print I use a sans-serif font called Verdana that is supposedly easier to read for someone who is sight-impaired. There are about a half dozen fonts out there that are recommended for large print. If you're going to go that route, I recommend researching it and making your own decision.

Ideally, your layout would have only one serifed font. That would mean your main body text, headers, etc. would be in that font and then you'd use a non-serifed, script, or decorative font for your chapter headers or other design elements.

For now, I'm going to break that rule since I already started with Bodoni for the title page and also by text. I suspect it wouldn't work for the main body so I'm going to use Garamond for that.

(All design experts are screaming in horror at this moment. The joys and dangers of self-publishing are that you can do anything you want.)

Getting back to our copyright notice. I'm changing the font to Garamond, Regular, 12 pt, and centering the text.

Now that we've chosen our font, we need to fix the copyright symbol. I wrote it as (c) and it stayed that way, which means I now need to go replace that with the appropriate glyph. To do so, highlight the (c) and go to Window→Text →Glyph Browser. That will bring up the Glyph Browser panel:

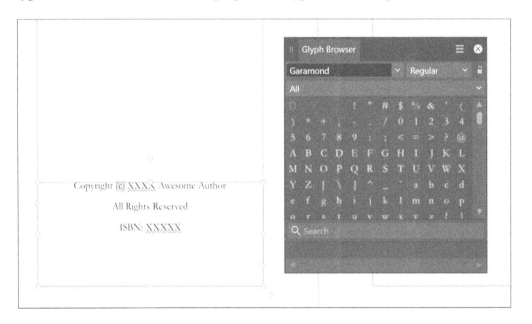

It should already be on the correct font (Garamond, Regular in my case). Scroll down until you find the copyright symbol written in that font and double-click on it. That will insert the symbol in place of your selected text.

Close the glyph browser.

While we're here, I also want to change the default spacing between those lines of text. Select the text and then go to the Paragraph panel in the top right and change the value for Leading at the top in the Spacing section. I changed mine to 14 point.

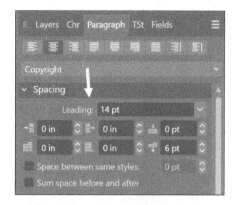

Next, we need a footer so we can include a page number for the chapter start page.

First step, click on the Frame Text Tool and insert a text frame on the bottom of the right-hand page in the margin area. I always make mine the same width as the text frame for the main text. Also, make sure it's tall enough to display your text in your chosen font size.

I also usually put it a little bit away from the main text frame, but not too close to the bottom of the page.

Click into the text frame and then go to the top menu and choose Text →Insert→Fields→Page Number.

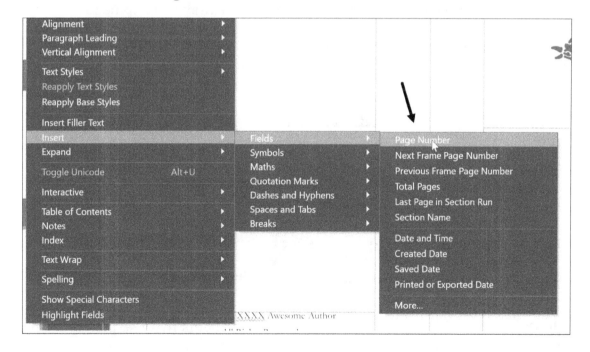

Affinity will insert a # sign into that text frame, which is the placeholder for the page number. Select All (Ctrl + A) and center the text. It should already be in Garamond, Regular, 12 point. If you want to use some other font, weight, or size, you could change that now.

If you prefer to have your page numbers on the outer edge of the page, which is recommended for large print, then the option you want to use is Align Away From Spine, which is in the dropdown menu in the dynamic menu at the top, or is the last option in the Paragraph panel row of icons.

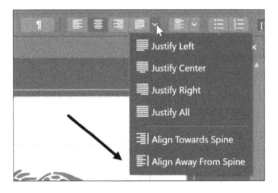

You don't want to use left or right alignment here, because that won't work on both the right- and left-hand pages. Choosing align away from spine saves a little effort and lets you just copy the footer when we move on to master pages that have the page number on both the left-hand and right-hand pages.

For me that's not a concern because I chose to center the page number.

I am also going to align the text in the text frame to the center of the frame top to bottom which is called Center Vertically.

The option is available in a dropdown to the right of the left, center, right, etc. options:

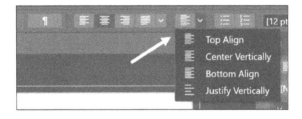

I do this because I have run into issues with documents that use picture frames and images where the text in my footer was impacted by the existence of those frames so that a right-hand page number didn't line up with a left-hand page number. Aligning the text to the center of the text frame fixed that issue.

Okay. Here we go:

We have our accent image. It's above our text frame where our main text will go. There's a text frame on the left-hand page that includes our copyright notice. And for the main body of the document we have a footer that includes a page number.

In the original version of this book I also showed my footer using accent images on either side of that number. You can insert those either using the glyph browser or by using a different font that has images available. This time around I'm just going to keep the footer simple.

The one thing I would suggest you don't try, because I have done this and it turned out to be annoying, is insert images in that footer text frame. You can do it. I did do it. But it was more trouble than it was worth.

Okay. On to the next master page. Let's do the No Text and Chapter Start page, because it's really easy to do from this point.

NO TEXT AND CHAPTER START
MASTER PAGE

For a novel, you will probably not need this master page. If you flip through most traditionally-published novels you'll see that the chapters generally start on whichever page is next. So sometimes the chapter starts on the left, sometimes on the right. There are no blank pages once things get going.

Where a No Text and Chapter Start master page is used is for non-fiction or short story collections. In both of those cases, it's more likely that each section, chapter, or story will start on the right-hand page. If there's not enough text to naturally make that happen, then you need a blank left-hand page to force it to happen.

So let's create that now.

Go to the Master Pages section of the Pages panel, Duplicate the Copyright and Chapter Start master page, rename it to No Text and Chapter Start, and then double-click on the thumbnail.

Next, go to the Layers panel, right-click on the text frame layer that is for the copyright notice, and choose Delete to remove that layer:

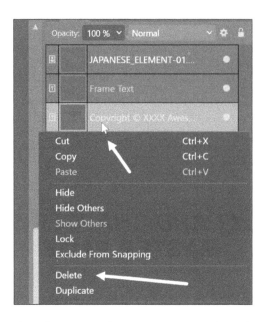

You can also click on that layer in the Layers panel and use the Delete key on your computer, at least on a PC.

Or you could choose the Move Tool and then click on the copyright text frame in your main workspace and use Delete, right-click and choose Cut, or use Ctrl + X.

Be sure if you try to do this directly in the document that the Move Tool is selected or you may end up deleting text instead of the text frame.

And there you have it:

Nothing on the left-hand page and a chapter start on the right-hand page. Easy peasy.

Alright, let's go ahead and create the rest of our master pages right now. It will feel like we're not doing much of anything, but what we're doing here is putting in place the framework that makes the rest of formatting a book much, much, much easier. So just stick with me on this.

TEXT AND CHAPTER START MASTER PAGE

The next master page we're going to create is the Text and Chapter Start master page. First, go to the Master Pages section of the Pages panel, Duplicate the No Text and Chapter Start master page, rename it, and double-click on the thumbnail to make sure it's the one showing in the main workspace. (You may at this point need to scroll down to find that thumbnail image in your Master Pages section.)

The right-hand page is already set up, so all we need to do is set up the left-hand page. That requires a header, a text frame, and a footer.

Let's start with the footer. Make sure the Move Tool (black arrow) is selected. Click on the footer on the right-hand page, use Ctrl + C to copy and Ctrl + V to paste, and then left-click and drag that copied footer over to the left-hand page and make sure that it lines up with the footer on the right-hand page as well as the text area on the left-hand page.

Like so:

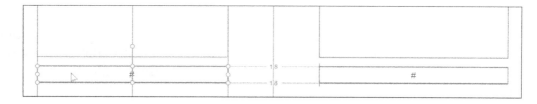

In the ebook or color edition you should be able to see the red and green lines that show that the new footer is aligned with the old one and the text area on the left-hand page. In the black and white print version you should see dark lines that show that alignment.

That's the footer. Easy enough.

Now let's put in our text frame. And I'll tell you why we're doing it in this order in a moment. So, click on the Frame Text Tool (the capital T), and then left-click and drag to create a text frame that fills the entire available space for text on the left-hand page, so overlaps the blue rectangle that's already there.

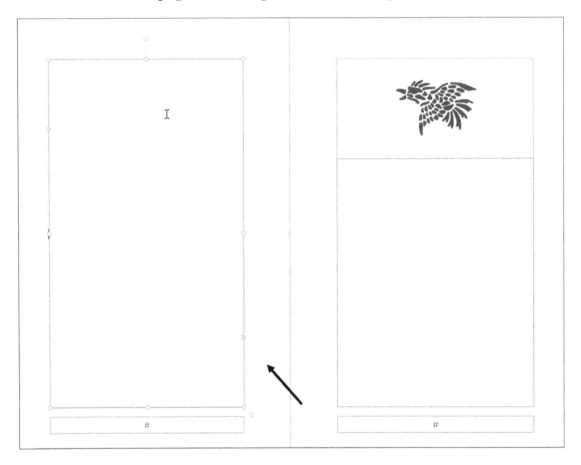

You can see above that my text frame is the same size and shape as the blue border underneath. If you do this right you'll only see one rectangle, but it will have the circles visible around the perimeter indicating that you're seeing a text frame.

Next, we need the header. Click on the Move Tool, click on the footer on the left-hand page, and then use Ctrl + C to copy and Ctrl + V to paste. (You can also right-click and choose Copy and Paste that way, but control shortcuts are quicker. If you're on a Mac, I believe you use Cmd.)

What I want you to do next is arrow up and then back down once and I want you to notice the value that Affinity displays above the text frame for the footer.

Here, for example, that is .174:

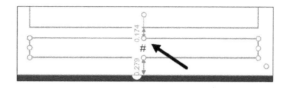

That number represents the distance from the top of the footer to the text frame where the main text will display. We want the header to be that same distance from the text. Or at least, that's how I like to do it.

Once you know that number, you can left-click and drag the copied footer up into the header area of the left-hand page and then position it so that the header is aligned to the text frame for the main body text and is the same distance above that frame as the footer is below it. I do this by aligning it on the left and right edges first and then using the up and down arrows to get that distance.

In this case I was able to get .173 above, which is close enough.

Once the header is in position, we need to change the contents. Right now it shows the page number, which needs to be removed, and we need to replace that with author name. Click on the Artistic Text Tool (the capital A), click into the frame, delete the # sign, and then go to the Fields panel, which we placed in the top right corner at the end.

Click on the space next to Author and it should turn white:

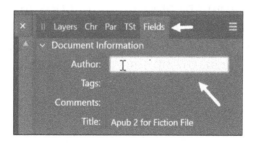

Type in the author name you want to use for the document and hit Enter. Double-click on the white text that says Author to the left of that. This will insert your author name into the header on your master page. (I wish it inserted as a field name <Author>, so you'd understand that this is a field and not text that was manually entered, but it doesn't.)

And, here you go:

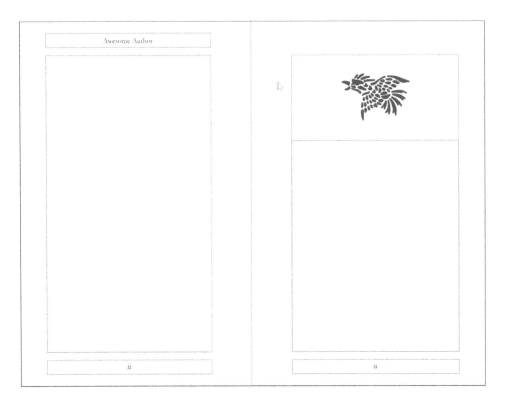

One Text and Chapter Start master page. But we have one more thing we need to do. And that's tell Affinity that the text from the left-hand page should flow to the right-hand page. This master page is for where a chapter ends and the next chapter starts and we're going to put our entire book into Affinity at once so we need our chapters to connect to one another.

The way to do this is to click on the left-hand text frame. When you do that, you'll see a very small blue arrow on the right-hand side of the frame.

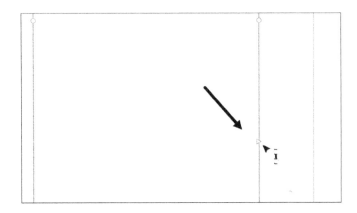

Click on that arrow and it will shade the entire text frame blue. Move your cursor over to the right-hand text frame, which will then also shade in blue:

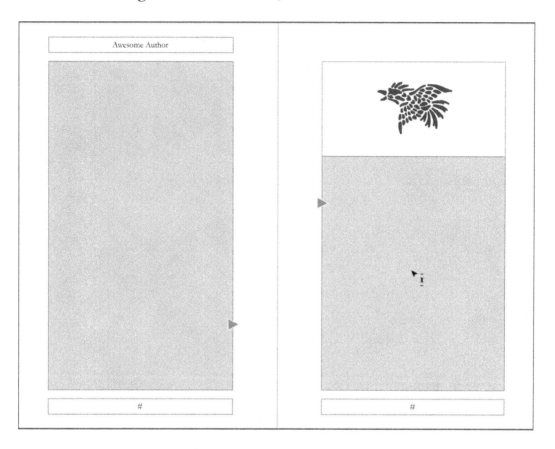

Click on the second text frame. You should now see a line that connects the two text frames with an arrow on that line pointing in the direction of the right-hand text frame. That indicates the direction the text will flow.

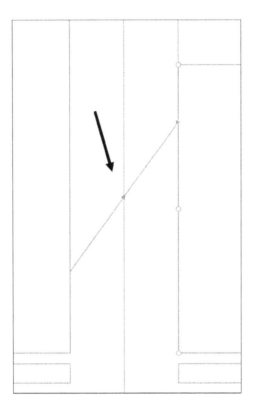

And now we're done with this one.

* * *

Quick note, Affinity is really good in my experience at generating recovery files, so if it ever crashes on you try to reopen the file you had open at the time and it will often have the file saved almost up to the moment it crashed. But I also currently have a pretty, shiny, new piece of you-know-what computer that randomly crashes on me a lot so I also recommend using Ctrl + S or saving regularly as you work on a project like this, just in case.

Second quick note, while we're taking a break here. The headers and footers I'm showing you in this book are one acceptable option. I wanted you to have a version that uses headers and footers so you could work with those. But you can do whatever you want.

I currently have six fiction titles sitting on my desk. (I read a lot and am too lazy to put things away.) Four of those titles have page number on the top outer edge of each page with author name on the left center top and title on the right center top of the page. So no footer. One has title on the left top, author on the right top, and page numbers on the bottom, all centered. The final one just has page numbers centered on the bottom and no title or author at all.

Those are all recent fiction books published by traditional publishers. The ones that don't have both a header and a footer probably did fit more text on those pages and cut down on number of pages printed by a small amount, so it may be worth experimenting with if that's a big concern for you.

At least when we're done here you should know enough about how to do these that you can configure it any way you want. Okay, on to the next.

TEXT AND TEXT MASTER PAGE

Our next master page is the Text and Text master page. This is the bread and butter of your book. Most of your book will likely be text and text pages, unless you have really short chapters (like I sometimes do).

First step, Duplicate the Text and Chapter Start master page that we just created and rename it. Double-click to make sure you have the right pages showing in the main workspace. (And, yes, I'm going to say that every time because of the number of times I have personally messed that up.)

Step one, delete the image. I did so using the Layers panel and the Delete key after I clicked on that layer.

Step two, click on the text frame for the right-hand page and click and drag the circle on the top of the frame until the text frame fills the entire space allowed for text, so overlaps the blue rectangle completely.

Step three, click on, copy, paste, and move the header from the left-hand page to the right-hand page until it is aligned with the text frame and the left-hand header.

If that doesn't work—in my case the header did not want to show alignment lines to the left-hand header—check the Transform panel value for the left-hand header to see the Y value and then change the Y value for the right-hand header to match.

Next, click onto the Artistic Text Tool and then into the frame for the right-hand header and delete the text there. Once that text is gone, go to the Fields panel and double-click on the white text that says Title. It will insert the title of your document into that header.

If you want the title to be different, click on the text for the title in the Fields panel and change it. The document will update automatically.

Be careful with long titles to make sure that they fit into the header text frame.

Finally, confirm that there is text flow from the left-hand page to the right-hand page. If not, connect the two text frames by clicking on the left-hand text frame, clicking on the blue arrow along the right-hand edge, and then clicking on the right-hand text frame.

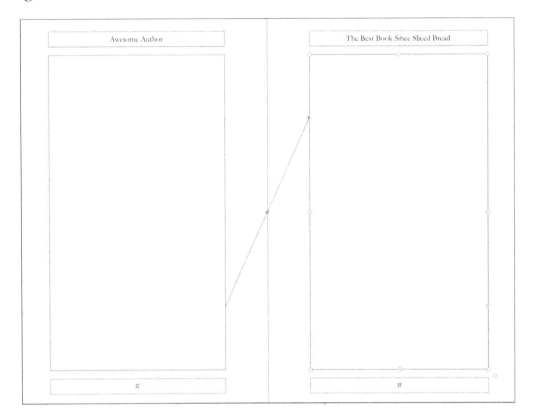

When you're done you should have something that looks like this: There are two text frames, a header on each page, a footer on each page, and the text will flow from the left-hand page to the right-hand page.

CHAPTER START AND TEXT MASTER PAGE

Now we need a master page for when a chapter starts on the left-hand side of the page. This is one that you'll want for most fiction books, but generally not need for non-fiction or short story collections.

For this one, go and Duplicate the Text and Chapter Start master page. Rename it. Double-click on the thumbnail.

The first thing we're going to do here is to insert the header on the right-hand page. There are a number of ways to do this. I am going to go to the Text and Text master page, copy the header on the right-hand page there, and then paste on this new master page. That pasted my header right where it needed to be and it had the book title already there.

That usually will work. But I've had it not work at times. Maybe because I didn't have the Move Tool selected, I don't know. If that option doesn't work, you can also duplicate the left-hand header, move the copy over, and then make sure the Y value matches up for both headers before deleting the left-hand one. You'd then also need to change the Author field and replace it with the Title field.

You could also just note the Y value for the left-hand header before dragging that header over to the right-hand page so you don't have to go back and delete anything.

Any of those options will work.

Next step, delete the left-hand header if it's still there. I click on it in the document and then go to the Layers panel and right-click and choose Delete from there.

Now we need to change our text frames. Click on the right-hand text frame and jot down the H and Y values in the Transform panel. Now click on the left-hand text frame and change the H and Y values in the Transform panel to match.

In this case, make sure that lock aspect ratio is NOT turned on so that the W value remains unchanged.

You should now have short text frames on both the left-hand and right-hand page and they should both be lined up along the bottom of the blue rectangle.

Move the image from the right-hand page to the left-hand page. When I just tried to do this on my page, the snapping lines wouldn't show how to center that image top to bottom in my space at the top of the page, so I had to Undo (Ctrl + Z) and record the Y value for the image from the Transform panel and then move the image again and make sure that my Y value was still the same on the left-hand page.

By doing that we make sure that the chapter start images are all at the same height as you flip through the book. Also, remember to use the correct center line so that you're centered in the blue rectangular space and not to the whole page, since the margins are not even.

Finally, we need to go to the right-hand page and change the text frame there to fill the entire rectangular space. And here we are:

You may be wondering why I didn't just drag the text frames to the other page. Easy enough to do, right? Left-click drag, align to the bottom on each page, done.

The reason that doesn't work is because you have text flow already set up. It was set to flow from the left-hand page to the right-hand page, which is what we want. But if I just click and drag the two text frames to the opposite page, that reverses the text flow. It makes it so that the text flows from the right-hand page to the left-hand one. That is not what you want, obviously.

But if that ever happens you can fix it.

What you need to do is remove the text flow and then redo it in the correct direction. To remove the text flow, click on the arrow for the "starting" text frame and then click back onto that "starting" text frame.

Here I've moved those two text frames we just did to the opposite page and you can see by the directional arrow between them that the text is going to flow from the right to the left.

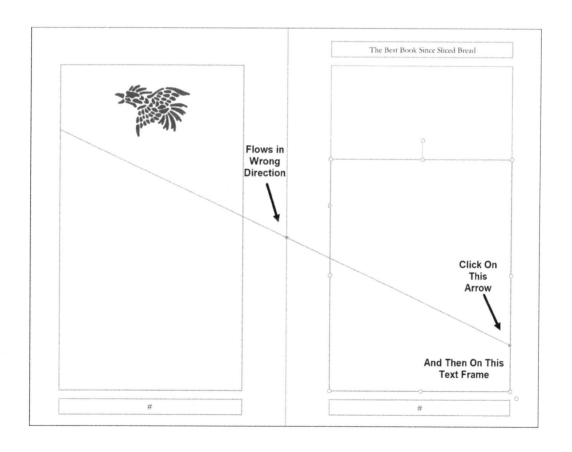

In this case you'd click on the arrow on the right-hand edge of the right-hand text frame and then click back onto that text frame. If you've done it right there should no longer be a flow line between the two text frames, and now you can create one that does go in the right direction.

But you can avoid having to do this by simply changing the heights of the text frames and leaving them in their original location.

Okay, on to the next.

TEXT AND ABOUT THE AUTHOR
MASTER PAGE

Now we're up to the end of the book. There are going to be two options that happen, depending on where your last chapter text ends. One is that it ends on the left-hand page, the other is that it ends on the right-hand page.

If it ends on the left-hand page then you'll want a Text and About the Author master page. (I've tried leaving that page blank and then putting the about the author on the next page, but it looks weird. You could do it. I think I actually had that in the last book. But ultimately it's better to just carry into something after that last page.)

If it ends on the right-hand page, I use a No Text and About the Author master page. One of the books in my stack of six here actually uses an About the Author on the left-hand side and then no more pages, but that looks really weird to me. (It's likely because in traditional publishing they have to print in groups of X pages, I think it's 8 but don't quote me on that, so they're always trying to finagle things to work with that, but for print-on-demand self-publishing, which is what most authors reading this book will do, that same issue does not exist.)

Okay. So Text and About the Author.

Duplicate the Text and Chapter Start master page. Rename. Double-click on the thumbnail. Also, for me, I'm going to left-click on that thumbnail and drag it to the end of the master page thumbnails. You'll see a blue line as you drag the thumbnail that will show where the thumbnail is going to move. Make sure that you drag it to the side of your existing master pages so that they all remain what they are and don't combine in weird ways.

To differentiate the About the Author page from the chapter headers, I'm going to move that accent image back over to the side like we had it on the title page, but keep it the same size as the chapters. At least for now. Once we have all of the text in there we may change things around.

Also, I'm going to delete the page number from the about the author side. I've seen this done both ways, but for me it's always the last page of the book even if I have back matter, so it doesn't need to be numbered and that's another subtle indication that the main story has ended.

So I click on and delete that footer.

Finally, we want to remove the text flow between the two text frames. To do that, click on the left text frame, click on the arrow on the right edge, and then click back onto the left-hand text frame.

(If you don't break that text flow, then you'll just need to remember that your about the author text is part of your main body text. I prefer to treat them separate, but it can work either way.)

Here we go:

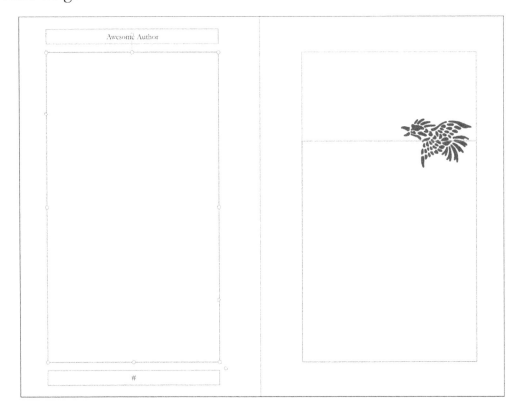

Now let's do the other one.

NO TEXT AND ABOUT THE AUTHOR
MASTER PAGE

This one will be very easy to do. Duplicate the Text and About the Author master page. Rename it. Double-click on the thumbnail. Delete everything from the left-hand page (header, footer, text frame.) Done.

BUILD THE START OF YOUR BOOK

Okay. Now that we have all the master pages we need, it's time to go back to the Pages section of the Pages panel and build our book.

The first page was already there and automatically formatted as a title page and then we added our text to it.

We also already added the Also By page. Right-click on the thumbnail for that one and choose Add Pages. We want 2 pages, After, Page 3, and the Master Page we want for this is Copyright and Chapter Start.

Make that selection and click OK.

Now right-click on that new thumbnail for Copyright and Chapter Start and choose to Add Pages again. This time choose Text and Text for the Master Page.

You should have four thumbnails that represent seven pages in your Pages section of your Pages panel:

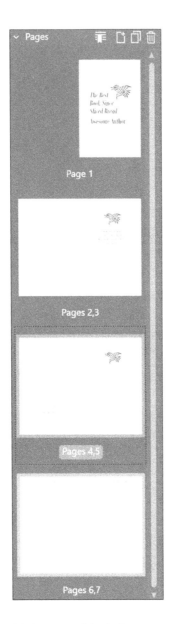

(A quick note here. You could have added four pages that first time when you right-clicked on the Also By page and then manually changed the master page for pages 6 and 7 after they'd already been added. We'll walk through how to do that later. But for me, this is the easiest way to build the front of the book.)

Okay. Next, double-click on the thumbnail for pages 4 and 5 or scroll up to them and you'll see that we have a problem to fix:

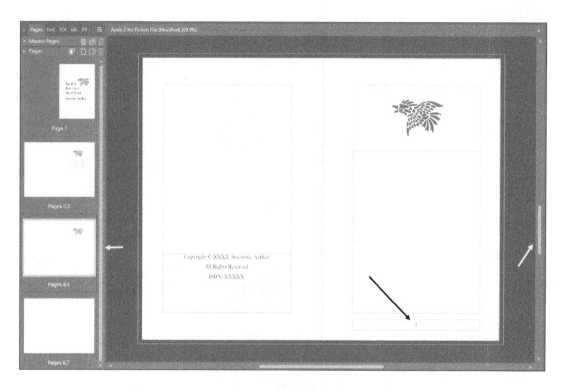

Affinity will by default treat your document as one section, which means that it starts any page numbering on the first page and moves forward. That results in our chapter start, which should be our page 1, being numbered page 5 instead.

To fix this, click on just the right-hand side of that thumbnail in the Pages section of the Pages panel, page 5. It should have a dark blue border around just that page if you did it correctly.

Right-click and choose Start New Section from the dropdown menu:

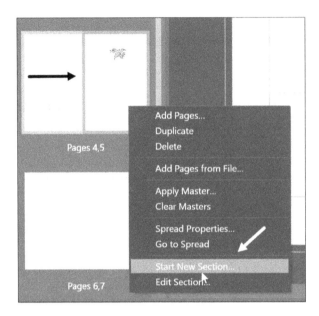

This will bring up the Section Manager dialogue box.

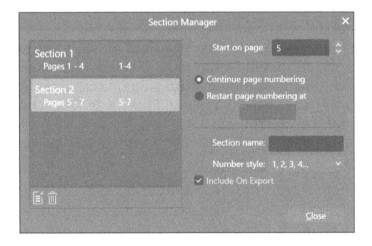

On the right-hand side of that dialogue box, change the option from Continue Page Numbering to Restart Page Numbering At by clicking on the black circle next to the restart option. The default for that should be 1, which is what we want.

Click Close and now the first chapter start will be numbered page 1. (We are using a very simple layout here, but this is also where you would go to have different numbering styles in different parts of your book or where you would assign section names if you were using those for chapter headers instead of the book title. That's covered in the next book in this series.)

One more thing we need to do here and that's flow text from page 5 to page 6 since those are different page spreads so we couldn't do that on the master pages.

In the main workspace scroll down so that the bottom of pages 4 and 5 show at the top and the top of pages 6 and 7 show at the bottom in the main workspace.

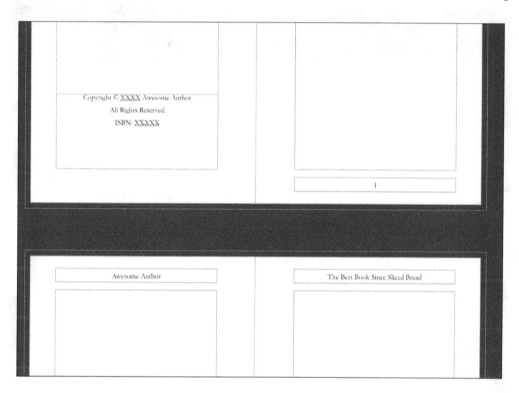

Copyright © XXXX Awesome Author
All Rights Reserved
ISBN: XXXXX

1

Awesome Author

The Best Book Since Sliced Bread

Like this:

Click on the text frame for page 5 (now numbered 1, our chapter start page). You should see the blue arrow on the right-hand edge that lets you flow text. Click on that arrow and then move your cursor to the text frame for page 6 and click on that.

Here I've clicked on the blue arrow already and it shaded the first text frame blue and now I have my cursor over the next text frame:

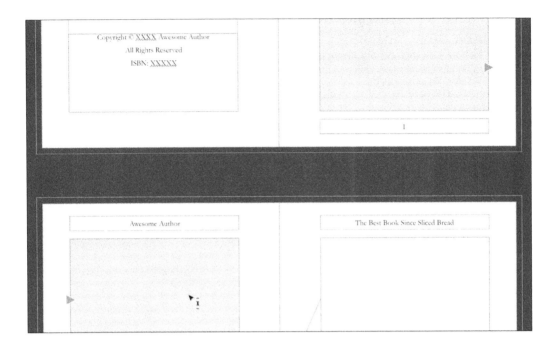

When I click on that second text frame, Affinity adds the flow line that shows that text will flow from that first master page to the next one.

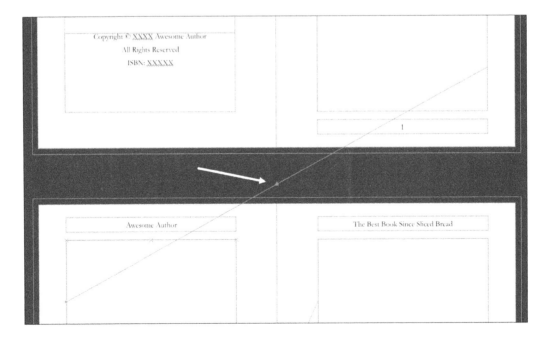

That should be the only time we have to do this. The rest will happen automatically when we add our text into the document and have Affinity add master pages for us.

Let's do that now.

ADD AND FLOW MAIN BODY TEXT

You should have the text of your book in a Word document, RTF file, or something similar. I personally do not recommend writing your book in Affinity Publisher. I think it is best used for your final formatting of your print book, but not for composition. And that's how I'm going to approach the rest of this book, with the assumption that you already wrote, edited, and finalized the text of your book elsewhere.

I personally use Microsoft Word. The only formatting I do is to use page breaks between my chapters, Heading 1 for chapter headers, and italics as needed. Everything else is formatted with the Normal style that's Word's default. But I have also used files that had text styles applied to each paragraph as well. Either one will work. But you don't have to get fancy in Word to bring that text into Affinity.

I also sometimes, if I've decided to format the ebook first, will export from Vellum as an .RTF file. That also works.

What you want from whatever source file you're using is to copy the main text of your document. Leave out any introductory text such as title, also by, etc. Also leave out any backmatter text such as an appendix, about the author, etc.

So, for example, when I export from Vellum I end up deleting the front and back matter first before I copy using Ctrl + A to select the remaining text and then Ctrl + C to copy it.

Once you have your main body text copied, go to your Affinity Publisher file. Make sure the Artistic Text Tool (the capital A) is selected. Next, click into the text frame on the first chapter page (so page 5 of the document that we've created so far) and paste the text (Ctrl +V or right-click, Paste).

If we did everything correctly up to this point, the text will automatically flow through from that page to the next two pages in your document, pages 6 and 7, which are numbered pages 2 and 3 and use your Text and Text master page:

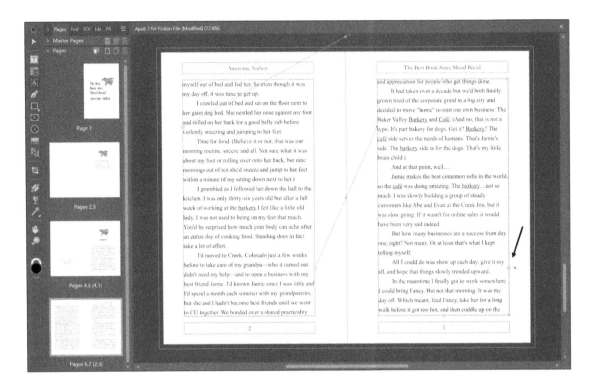

You will then see at the very end of that last page that the blue arrow for flowing text is red. What that indicates is that there is more text that you pasted into this document than there is space to flow that text to. The text is all there, but Affinity basically hides it behind the scenes.

This is very important to understand, especially if you're someone like me who is used to working in a program like Word where if you paste 200 pages of text, you get a 200-page document.

In Affinity that text exists, even when you can't see it, unless you deliberately delete it or delete all pages it is attached to.

That little red arrow is telling us there's more text and that we need to add more pages to our document to see it.

Now, one of the beautiful, wonderful, amazing things that Affinity does is it will flow your text and add new master pages for you until all of your text is visible. It can only do this from the last page of your document, though. And it does it based upon the last master page layout you used.

That's why I had you add a Text and Text master page instead of just working from the Copyright and Chapter Start master page. Because the Text and Text master page is probably going to be your most-commonly-used master page, so might as well apply that one to all of your text now and then you only have to change your master page spread for each new chapter start.

Okay. Let's do this so you can see how it works.

Hold down the Shift key and click on that red arrow. (If you're not seeing a red arrow but a red circle instead, click on the circle first to turn it into the arrow and then Shift and click on the arrow.)

Affinity should then add as many pages to the Pages section of the Pages panel to accommodate all of the text you pasted in. I used a fairly short book for this (about 40K words), but here is my last page:

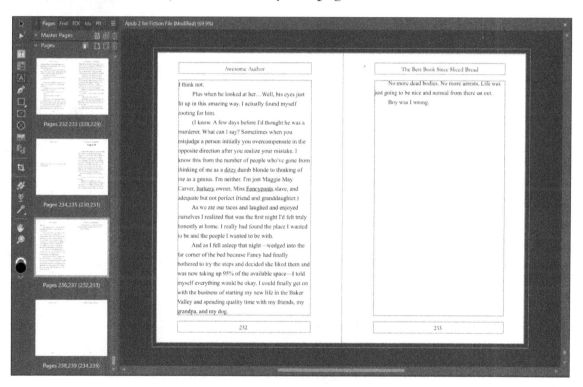

You can see that my document now has 239 pages in it. (Those last two pages are blank, likely because there was a page break at the end of the last chapter that I didn't delete.)

Affinity flowed that text and added those master pages for me in about twenty seconds, maybe less. Which is great, because I didn't have to guess how many pages I needed nor did I need to worry about flowing text between the pages I added. Affinity did all of that for me.

Which means all I have to do now for the main body is format my text, assign a different master page format to those pages where I have a chapter start, and then address issues like widows, orphans, and italics.

Once I've done all that I'll end with my About the Author page.

TEXT STYLES

Up to this point we have manually formatted our text. We haven't had a lot of it, so that was pretty easy to do and I didn't want to bog us down in a discussion of text styles so early on. But for the main body of your document, text styles are essential because they will save you a tremendous amount of time.

Think of a text style as a shortcut that has a font, font size, font style, and other attributes already stored. When you apply that style to your text, it applies all of those attributes to your text for you so that you don't have to go and choose the font, font size, etc. over and over again.

This means your formatting is more consistent, because you don't format one paragraph one way and the next a slightly different way.

It also saves a lot of time to use a text style. You can apply it with a click of a button or a Ctrl shortcut rather than have to hunt down all of the various settings.

For a basic novel or short story collection, you will have four potential text styles to create for the main body text:

1. Chapter Title

2. First Paragraph

3. Main Body Paragraph

4. Separator

In some of my non-fiction I have more than that because I have subheaders or sub-subheaders or numbered lists or bulleted lists, etc. But for a basic title, that should be it.

Let's create each of those now. I'm going to go back to the start of chapter 1 because three of the four occur on that first page.

CHAPTER TITLE

In general, your chapter title should be in a larger font size than the main body text. Often it will be in a different font as well. This is where a sans-serif or decorative font can be used for a special appearance.

I tend to name my chapters Chapter 1, Chapter 2, etc. but most of the books sitting here on my desk just use 1, 2, 3, etc. when that's the way the chapters are named. For me, keeping the word chapter in there lets me apply my chapter title format more easily, so I'm going to leave it.

But let me make sure real quick that I don't use the word chapter anywhere else. To do that, I'm going to go to the Find and Replace panel, type "chapter" into the Find field and then click on Find.

Here are the results:

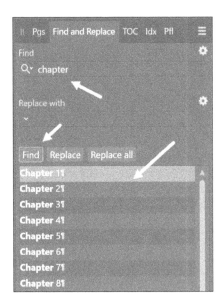

The entire list of results are all chapter names. I have no entries where it says something like, "this is the worst chapter of my life." Good.

Now let's come up with a format to use for those chapter headers. I'm going to increase my font size to 30 and choose a font I have called Fountain Rough. It's a script font with a texture to it so you'd never use it for the main body text in a novel, but it can work on a book cover or, in this case, at the top of chapters.

I'm not madly in love with it, but we'll keep it for now.

I also need to go to the Paragraph panel on the top right, because right now there is a very large space between the chapter title and the first paragraph. This is because of how the text was formatted when I brought it in from my RTF file:

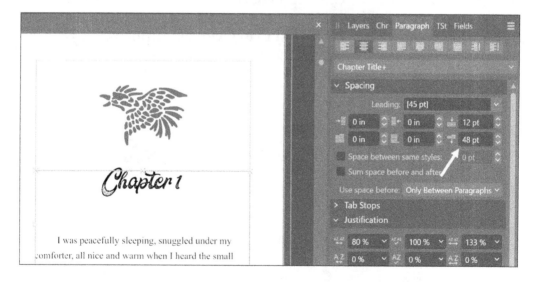

The value I want to change is that 48 on the right-hand side in the second row that's for the Space After Paragraph. It's fine to have it be more than the font size we're going to use (which will probably be 10 or 12 pt), but 48 is just a bit too much there. I think I want 24. As you enter different values, you'll see the text adjust:

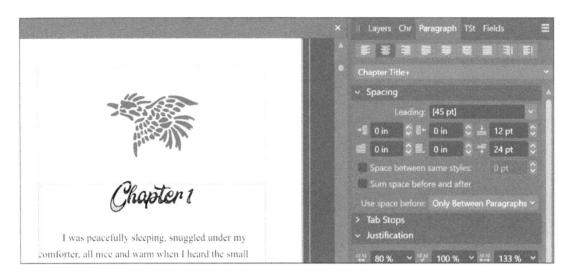

Okay. That's better. All of our chapters in this book will be one line only so I don't need to worry about that Leading value, but if I had chapter names (like I do in non-fiction) that were going to wrap to the next line I'd want to probably change that value as well.

(You can update a style later if needed, so we're not locked into this, but it's best to finalize your styles before you start walking through the document page-by-page and applying master pages and fixing widows, orphans, etc.)

Now that we have our format for the chapter title, let's turn it into a text style. To do that, select the text and go to the Paragraph Style dropdown menu in the dynamic menu up top:

It is the second style dropdown menu, not the first.
(You could also use the Text Styles panel, but that's never the way I do it.)
Choose New Style. That will open the Create Paragraph Style dialogue box:

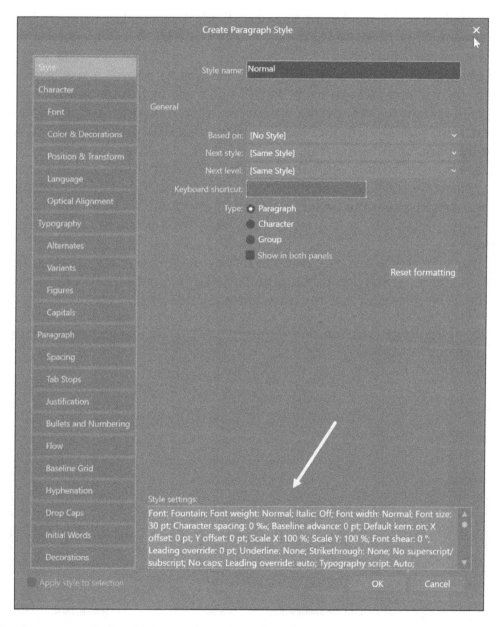

At the bottom of the dialogue box is a description of everything that Affinity thinks creates that style. You can see the font type listed there, that it's not italic, that it's 30 pt, etc. Don't worry too much about that for this one, but it'll be useful to know about that in a moment.

In the Style Name field, type a name for your style. Mine is going to be Chapter Title

Also, click into the Keyboard Shortcut field. What makes using styles speed things up is having shortcuts assigned to each one so that you can just use that shortcut to apply the style.

For me, and this is not necessarily the best way to do this, I use Shift + 1, 2, 3, 4, etc. for my text style shortcut keys. It gets me in trouble at times if I find that I need to edit text in my document and that I need to use an exclamation point, at sign, pound sign, etc. Because I try to use a pound sign and instead change my paragraph formatting.

But since I use Affinity Publisher primarily for formatting and not writing or editing, those are the keyboard shortcuts I use because the keys are very easy to reach and keeping them in order (1 for chapter title, 2 for first paragraph, 3 for main body paragraph, 4 for separator, etc.) makes them easy for me to remember.

Choose what works for you. But whatever you choose, click into that box and use the shortcut. Affinity will then populate that box with the shortcut you used like it did here with Shift + 1 for my Chapter Title style:

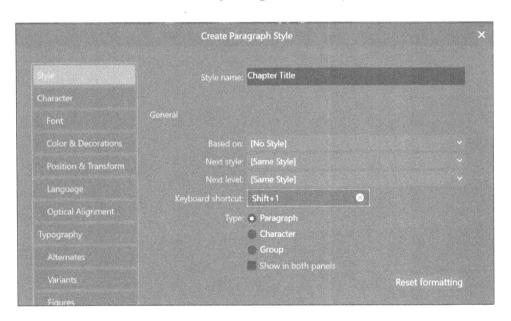

Click OK and now you have that style to use.

FIRST PARAGRAPH

Next let's create our first paragraph style. This is the style to use at the start of each chapter or the start of each section.

I'm now down to five sample novels on my desk. All five have a first paragraph of the chapter that is not indented. Three of the five also don't indent the first paragraph after a break, two do.

I should also note that four of the five that I just looked at use a drop cap for the first letter of the first paragraph in the chapter, but we're not going to get that fancy here.

Okay.

I'm going to use Garamond for the font. No paragraph indent. 12 pt. Regular. Justify Left. And use hyphenation as well. (Five of five in my little sample stack here use justify left, four of the five use hyphenation.)

Another option for paragraph formatting would be left-aligned which leaves a ragged margin on the right-hand side. That's what I do for large print, along with no hyphenation, because it ensures that all words are equally spaced and that someone doesn't have to struggle to follow the word to the next line.

And, actually, often in my regular print books I will do justified left and no hyphenation and just fix weird gaps with a little tracking adjustment because I seem to have something against hyphenation, but that's not the norm.

(Sometimes, because I am a creature of chaos at heart, I'll just use hyphenation on one little line or paragraph where I used a really long word and there's no good way to fix it without using hyphenation. Don't be me.)

Okay. So. Let's make these changes to the first paragraph of the document. Select the text. Font and font size happen in the dynamic menu up top.

Next, we can go to the Paragraph panel. I'm going to make the Leading 14 here. That's the space between the lines. I'm also going to make the space after the paragraph 0. Hyphenation is in a section lower down in that panel. We just need to check auto-hyphenation. I also expand Baseline Grid and make sure Align To Baseline Grid is turned off.

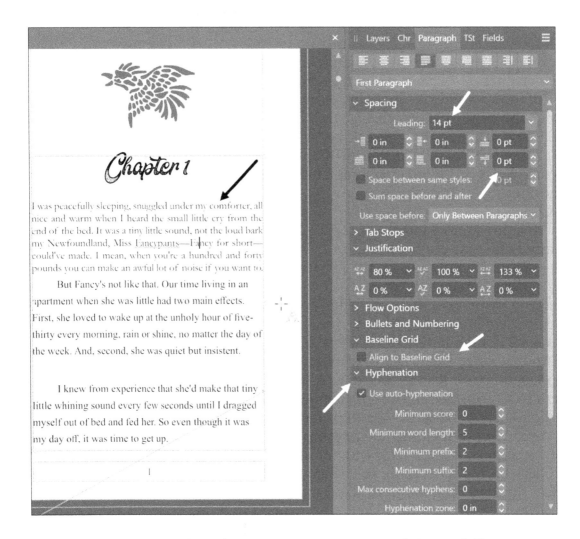

You can also expand the Flow Options section and have Affinity prevent orphans and widows for you, which is what I do for large print. But for regular print books I prefer to do that manually, because sometimes I can tweak the spacing in an earlier paragraph on a page to bring a line up and eliminate the orphan or widow that way, which ensures that my text starts and ends at the same point on facing pages.

(We'll cover that more in the chapter on fixing widows and orphans.)

Great. Done. Now let's add that as a new style. I'm going to use the shortcut Shift + 2 for this one.

MAIN BODY PARAGRAPH

The main body paragraph style is really easy to create, because it's just the First Paragraph style with an indent added to it.

So I'm going to click on that second paragraph there and use Shift + 2 to apply my first paragraph style to it and then change the indent for the first line to .2. Here it is:

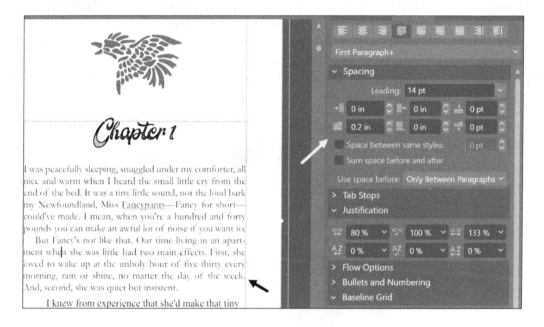

Once more, we can go to the paragraph style dropdown menu to create a new style here, but before we do that, I want to show you something:

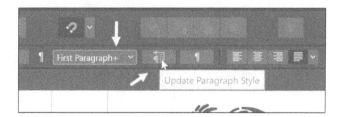

Note how that says First Paragraph+ for the paragraph style name. This is how Affinity indicates that you took a paragraph style, First Paragraph, and modified it. So it's telling me that the paragraph of text that I'm currently clicked into is not actually formatted using that style. It started with that style, but I changed it.

Which we know, because we did so deliberately. But if I had done so because I wanted to change the First Paragraph formatting, then I'd need to do one more thing to update that particular style to incorporate my changes. And that is to click on the Update Paragraph Style option to the right of the dropdown. If I click on that option, Affinity will update my First Paragraph style to reflect my changes.

So, for example, just a moment ago, you didn't see this, but I initially had a 14 pt value for the space after my paragraph. But I realized I needed that to be zero. So I changed the value to zero and then just clicked on Update Paragraph Style to incorporate that into my existing style I'd just created.

Okay. Here, though, we want to create a new style so we click on the dropdown arrow to make that New Style choice.

That gives me this Create Paragraph Style dialogue box which I've filled in with my style name and shortcut:

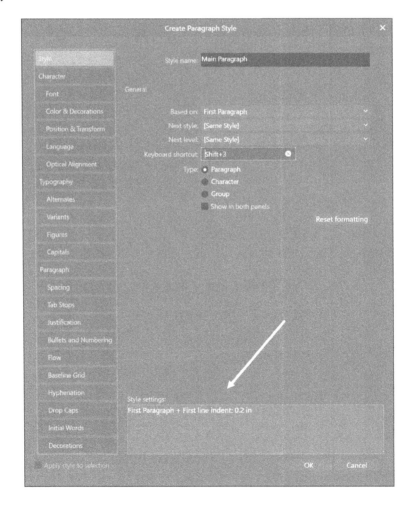

Look at the bottom there where it says Style Settings. Instead of the long paragraph listing all of the possible settings that we saw for First Paragraph, this one just says "First Paragraph + First line indent: .2 in."

Basically what that is saying is that my Main Paragraph style is the First Paragraph style with a change to the first line indent. Any change I make to the First Paragraph style will also apply to this style, except for any change made to the paragraph indent.

So let's say I decided I wanted to use Baskerville URW for my font. I only have to make that change to the First Paragraph style.

Or let's say I decide I want to use a 10 pt font instead of 12 pt. Same thing, I only need to change the First Paragraph style.

My chapter title style, however, remains completely separate.

What I usually end up with is one style grouping for my accent elements and another grouping for my main text elements. So I format one style in each group and then apply that style to any other text in my document that should be part of that group and edit from there. That way I can easily modify the entire group by going to the "base" style, in this case First Paragraph for my main text elements.

We sort of cheated here and I didn't make you use text styles for the front matter of this book so that text is not tied into the main text right now, but we'll clean that up in the next chapter.

For now, let's save this as a new style, Main Paragraph, with a shortcut of Shift + 3.

Next, let's create a style for our paragraph separators.

SEPARATOR STYLE

Here is a page where I have a couple of separated sections within a chapter:

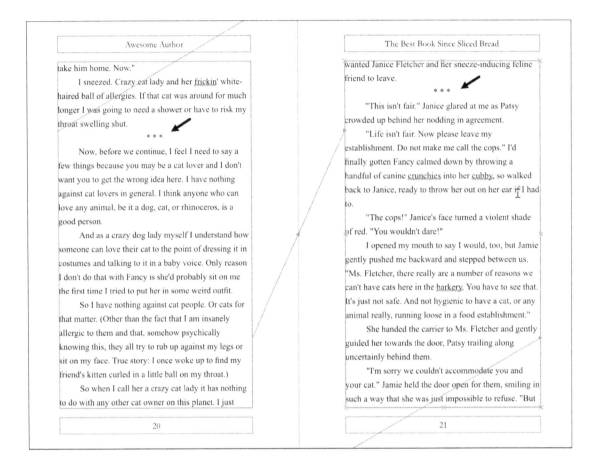

As I write I just use * * * to create these separations. Sometimes I leave it that way in the final version. In my cozy mysteries I change the font over to Ennobled Pet so that they're little paw prints. A non-fiction book I'm reading right now uses a little image of books on a shelf. Some books use a blank line (although be careful there because you'll probably need to use something if that break falls at the top or bottom of a page).

If you do use an image, it takes more effort to position the image correctly. I prefer to use a font that has embellishments as part of the font to get that effect, because then Affinity treats that like text and centers it for me automatically. Fonts like Wingdings come with a lot of shapes that you can use.

For this one, let's use the Ennobled Pet font to get our result. (It's a free font you can download.) First, though, I want to apply my paragraph formatting to the paragraphs before and after the section break so I can see what it will look like. So Shift + 3 for the paragraph above, Shift + 2 for the paragraph after.

Since this is going to be a different font and font size, I'm just setting it up standalone. If it were more tied into the settings I used for First Paragraph I could apply that style first and then work from there like I did for the Main Paragraph style.

Here it is with the Ennobled Pet font, 14 pt, with 0 pt above and 8 pt below:

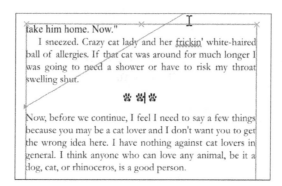

I think that works, but I want to test it on the other separator on this page to see if that top spacing is only working because the last line of the paragraph is short.

I could create a new style for this right now and then use my shortcut to apply the style to that other separator, but let me take this opportunity to show you the Style Picker tool that is available in Affinity Publisher 2.0 but was not available in the original program.

The Style Picker Tool lets you take the style on a selection and apply it to another one. I think you can do this with any object, but so far I've just used it for text.

The Style Picker Tool can be found in the secondary menu for the Color Picker Tool. So click the little white arrow next to the Color Picker Tool and then click on Style Picker Tool:

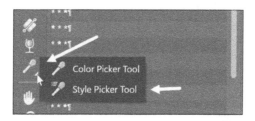

Your cursor will look like an eyedropper. When the eyedropper is angled towards the right, that's when you can select a style:

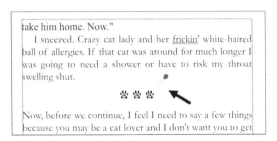

As soon as you select the style you want to copy by clicking on that text, the eyedropper will angle in the other direction.

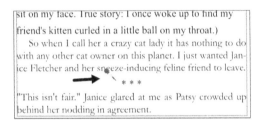

You can then select the text or object you want to apply that style to. Use the Esc key to switch it back to copy mode if needed. The style will apply one character at a time with text, so be sure to select all of your text.

That's how I just applied the format I created here to the second set of separators on this page:

ake him home. Now."

    I sneezed. Crazy cat lady and her frickin' white-haired ball of allergies. If that cat was around for much longer I was going to need a shower or have to risk my throat swelling shut.

🐾 🐾 🐾

Now, before we continue, I feel I need to say a few things because you may be a cat lover and I don't want you to get the wrong idea here. I have nothing against cat lovers in general. I think anyone who can love any animal, be it a dog, cat, or rhinoceros, is a good person.

    And as a crazy dog lady myself I understand how someone can love their cat to the point of dressing it in costumes and talking to it in a baby voice. Only reason I don't do that with Fancy is she'd probably sit on me the first time I tried to put her in some weird outfit.

    So I have nothing against cat people. Or cats for that matter. (Other than the fact that I am insanely allergic to them and that, somehow psychically knowing this, they all try to rub up against my legs or sit on my face. True story: I once woke up to find my friend's kitten curled in a little ball on my throat.)

    So when I call her a crazy cat lady it has nothing to do with any other cat owner on this planet. I just wanted Janice Fletcher and her sneeze-inducing feline friend to leave.

🐾 🐾 🐾

"This isn't fair." Janice glared at me as Patsy crowded up

I think I still like that spacing, so let me turn that into a new paragraph style with the shortcut of Shift + 4. Done.

* * *

Now we can go do a little quick clean-up to tie our front matter text and headers and footers into the First Paragraph text style. You don't have to do this next part, I'm just going to show you, because it will make changing your document font later much easier to do.

FRONT MATTER TEXT STYLE CLEAN-UP

In order to create a template where all of my text is nestled under the First Paragraph style, I'm going to go back now and quickly fix my front matter and master pages. If you don't care about this, you don't have to do it. Just keep in mind that you'll need to manually adjust those front matter sections if you ever change your main body font.

First step, go to the Pages panel and expand the Master Pages section. We're just going to work our way down through the thumbnails in that section.

On the Also By page I've decided to switch that over to use Garamond so that it matches the rest of the book. To do that, I select the header text, apply the First Paragraph text style (Shift + 2) and then bold, Align Center, change the font size to 16 pt, and add an 8 pt space after.

Save that as Also By Header text style.

Next, select the book titles, Shift + 2 to apply the First Paragraph text style, Align Center, use a 6 pt space after.

Save that as Also By Titles text style.

Move on to the copyright and chapter start page. Select the copyright text. Shift + 2. Align Center. 6 pt space after each line. Save as Copyright text style.

Finally, go to the footer that has the pound sign. Select it. Shift + 2 to apply the First Paragraph text style. Align Center. Center Vertically. Save as Header and Footer text style with a shortcut of Shift + 5.

Go through the rest of the master pages and apply the Header and Footer style to the headers and footers using Shift + 5. (This is admittedly one of those times when having just one-page master pages would save time, but it still only took me about two minutes to do.)

And done.

Now if I ever decide that I want to change the font used throughout my document, I can do so by just changing the First Paragraph text style.

And, actually, any attribute I didn't specifically change for one of the other styles that I change for the First Paragraph text style will apply to those styles as well.

Just do watch out if you change font size, such as for large print, because you will have to manually adjust any of the dependent text styles that had a font size specified, such as the Also By Header text style.

* * *

If you ever want to see which text styles are the main text styles that others are based off of, go to the Text Styles panel and use the three bars at the end of the panel tab listing to change the view to Show Hierarchal. (The default view is to show them alphabetically.)

That will collapse the styles down to the primary style and then you can expand a style to see the ones that are based on that style. Like here where you can see that I've expanded First Paragraph and there are five styles indented and listed underneath it:

* * *

Okay. Now let's go apply styles to our main body text.

APPLY STYLES

Since the large majority of the text in the main body of a document is going to be the Main Paragraph text style, that's the first style I assign to all of my text in the main body of my document.

So I click into the text frame for the start of Chapter 1, use Ctrl + A to select all of the main body text, and then use Shift + 3 to apply my Main Paragraph text style to all of it.

I get something like this on that first page:

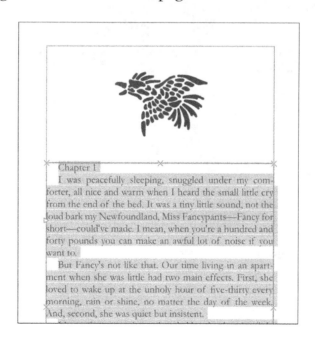

Now all I have to do is go through and apply chapter title, first paragraph, and separator formatting when it's needed.

Depending on how you named your chapters or how you format your separators, there may be a few shortcuts you can use for this.

CHAPTER TITLES

Because my chapter titles are all Chapter [X] and I didn't use the word chapter anywhere else in the book, I can use the Find and Replace panel to format my chapter headers.

To do this, I go to the Find and Replace panel and type "chapter" in the Find field.

Next, I click on the little gear widget next to Replace With and use the Paragraph Style secondary dropdown menu to choose Chapter Title.

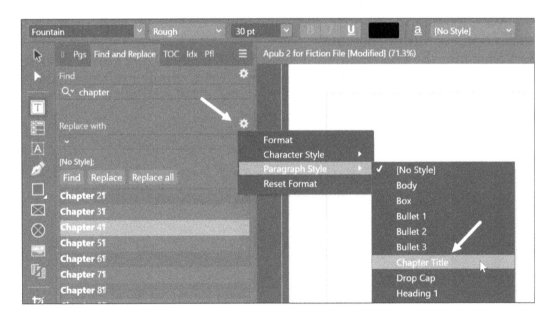

Finally, I click on Find and then on Replace All.

You can click through on a couple of entries to see that each chapter header now has that style applied to the text:

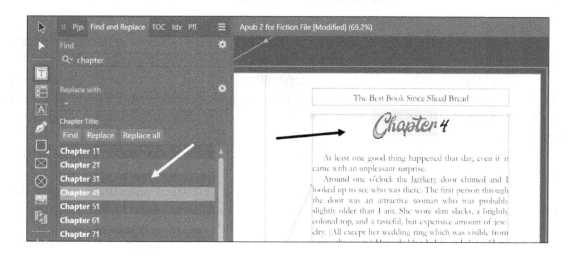

Note that it didn't just apply to the word "chapter", but also applied to the number. That's because this is a paragraph style and it applies to the entire "paragraph" even when that paragraph is just one line.

Separators

I can do something similar with my separators since I only use * * * for that purpose. (At least in that book.)

This time I look for * * * and replace with the Separator paragraph style.

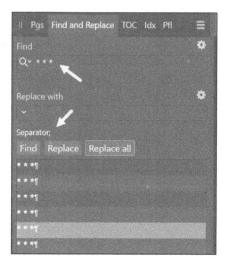

FIRST PARAGRAPHS

I like to remove the indent from the first paragraph after a separator, which means I need to apply my First Paragraph text style to those paragraphs.

I can use the search results for my separators to locate each one by clicking on each search result for * * * in the Find and Replace panel. Then I can click into the main document on the paragraph below each separator and apply that First Paragraph text style.

It's easier to do it this way than to walk through the document so I don't miss one, which can be easy to do.

After that, if I wanted, I could search again for "chapter" and do the same for the first paragraph of each of my chapters. Although that one I usually apply as I walk through the document and apply my master pages. Either way works.

DOUBLE-CHECK TIME

The next big step is going to be walking through the entire document and making any little tweaks for widows, orphans, weird spacing, etc. while also applying our master pages for each chapter.

But before we do that it's time to take a moment and see if everything looks okay.

Do you like the amount of space between your chapter headers and the first line of text? Do you like the spacing between paragraphs? Between lines? Do you like the spacing around your separators? Do you like the placement of any image you used? What about your headers and footers?

Anything else that needs fixed now? Because if you decide later that you don't like it, you'll have to do a lot of duplicate work. So this is the moment to get any of that fixed if you want it fixed.

The reason to figure this all out now is because the spacing of elements and text on the page will impact where your chapters end, which will impact which master page to apply.

Also, the spacing impacts whether you have widows or orphans that you need to deal with. If I have an 8 pt space between my chapter title and my first line of text, that will create different widows or orphans than if I have a 16 pt space.

So work all of that out now. Make sure your elements are what you want them to be before you move forward.

During this process I noticed an issue with my Text and Text master page:

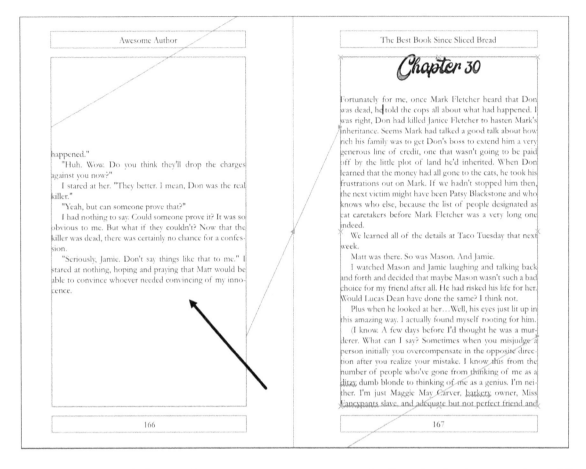

The text in that left text frame is set to center vertically. We don't want that. All of the text frames for text need to be set to Top Align. So I went back through my Master Pages section of my Pages panel and checked my text frames to make sure they all use Top Align instead of Center Vertically.

That's something that really only shows itself when there's text in the text frame and it's not enough to fill it. This particular issue doesn't impact where lines fall on the page, but it's still good to fix it as soon as you notice it.

Okay, so double-check. Make sure everything looks "good". Fix it if you need to. And then we can continue.

WIDOWS, ORPHANS, AND OTHER ISSUES

Widows and orphans are single lines alone at either the top or bottom of the page. Here you can see examples of one of each:

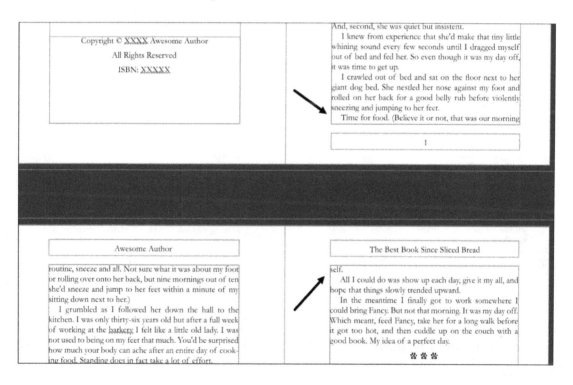

Ideally, you try to avoid having either one. But sometimes, you just can't. Like here, that top one where there's a single line at the bottom of the page, I have no good options for fixing that. I could force that line to the next page if I wanted, but I really don't, so I'm just going to leave it.

But I absolutely do not like that "self" at the top of page 3. Especially because it's part of a hyphenated word.

The way I try to fix widows and orphans is I try to identify a paragraph earlier on that page or the prior page where I can pull text up one line.

Especially when I'm not using hyphenation this is often possible because justifying text can put extra space between words to make the text reach the end of the line.

Here's what I have to choose from:

The best candidate on this one is actually the last paragraph that's falling over to the next page. So I'm going to select that text, go to the Character panel, and click on the dropdown for Tracking:

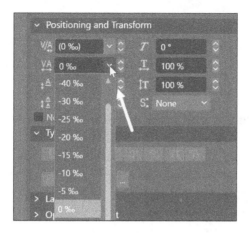

I hold my mouse over each of those negative values starting with -5% and stopping around -20%. Beyond that the text starts to look too cramped.

In this case, -5% brought the rest of that line back up to the prior page:

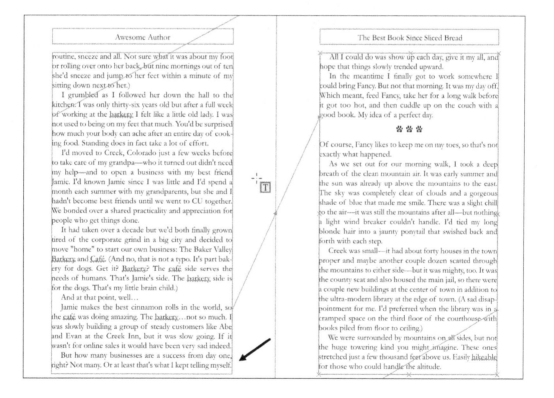

You really can't see any difference between that paragraph and the ones around it and now we don't have that little "self" carrying through to the next page.

Great. I'll continue through the document looking for lines like that that can be fixed. You have to do this from first chapter to last, because the changes you make to adjust one widow, orphan, or other line issue will impact all other lines in that chapter.

Other things to watch for are paragraphs that end with one really short word alone on a line. I believe the guidance is three letters or less. So if a line ends with just the word "too" you want to try to pull that up to the prior line.

If you use hyphenation, watch out for any scenario where too many words are hyphenated in a row. I think that's called pig bristles. Affinity lets you tell it the maximum number of consecutive hyphens. The default looks to be zero. But you could still have a scenario with say three out of five lines in a paragraph hyphenated that wouldn't look good on the page.

Try not to have a chapter end with just one line on the final page. Two lines on the last page you can maybe get away with. Three or more is better.

Also pay attention to any situation where the same word is on three lines in a row at the same spot. (Rare, but I think I've seen it once.)

And, if you're not using hyphenation but are justifying your paragraphs, look out for unseemly white space on the page where words have been spaced out too much on a line.

This is one of those times where reading a lot in print is a benefit because things will be jarring when they look wrong.

Now let's talk about the other adjustment you need to make at the same time, and that's applying your master pages for chapter starts.

APPLYING MASTER PAGES

The way we had Affinity flow our text through the entire document was by letting it use the Text and Text master page throughout. But that's not the master page you want to have for your chapter starts. So each time you reach a new chapter, you need to apply a different master page.

This requires you to make a decision. Do you want your chapter starts to fall where they may, on the left or right as the case may be? Or do you always want your chapters to start on the right-hand page? You need to make that decision now.

Because, here, is our first chapter that we need to change:

Depending on what you decide, it's either going to look like this:

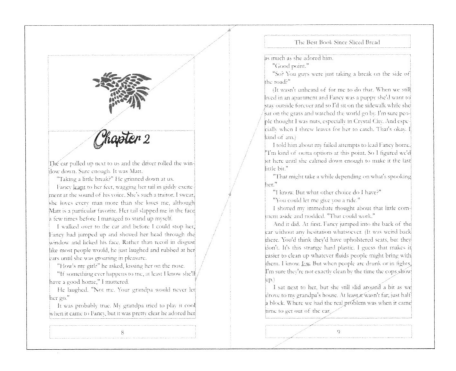

Or like this:

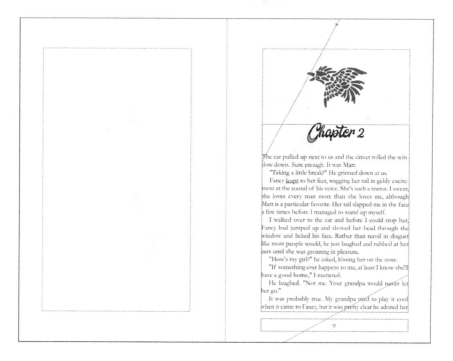

You can see that the decision you make has a profound impact on where your text falls, especially across three hundred pages or more of text.

So make that decision now. We are going to use the "let it fall where it may approach" for this novel. So we need to apply the Chapter Start and Text master page to this two-page spread.

To do that, go to the Pages section of the Pages panel and locate the thumbnail for these pages:

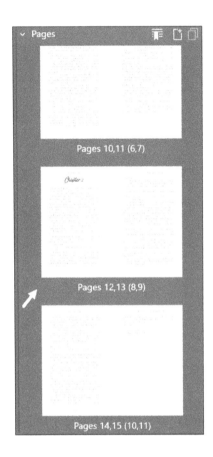

The advantage to applying your chapter title style first is that it makes it easier to see in the thumbnail so you can easily locate those pages. But even if you don't have that, you should know your page numbers, and you can see below each thumbnail the page numbers in the overall document as well as the page numbering for that section in parens.

So here we were looking for pages 8 and 9 and we can see that it's shown as "Pages 12, 13 (8,9)". Click on that thumbnail.

Be sure that you have chosen both pages in the thumbnail, not just one of the two. The whole thumbnail should be surrounded by a blue box.

Right-click and choose Apply Master from the dropdown menu.

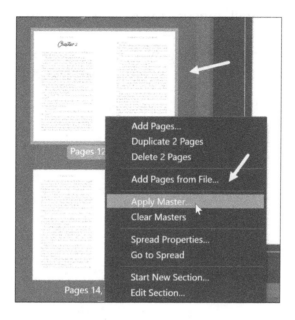

The Apply Master dialogue box will appear:

Use the dropdown at the top to choose the master page you want. They'll be listed in the order you have them in the Master Pages section of the Pages panel. Click OK.

That two-page spread will now use the master page you chose and the text will reflow appropriately.

Move forward from there dealing with widows, orphans, etc. and applying your master pages for each chapter until you reach the end of the document.

ITALICS AND BOLDED TEXT

The great thing about using text styles is that you can format most of your text in less than five seconds. The bad thing about using text styles is that when you do that you lose any italics or bolding or other special formatting that you used for individual words in that text.

I save this step for the end because I don't use italics that much. If you have whole paragraphs of text in italics, you may want to include this step with your walkthrough of the document to apply styles and master pages because italics do take up a different amount of space than plain text, so can shift your text slightly. Usually when it's one or a handful of words, it's not a big issue. But if you have whole paragraphs in italics, do that formatting as you walk through the document.

What I do, though, is wait until the end and then use the search function to locate the text I need to italicize. You'll need to search in your source document for any italics and then locate that same text in Affinity and apply italics to it.

In Word, use Ctrl + H to open the Find and Replace dialogue box, go to the Find tab, and then click into the Find What box, and use Ctrl + I. It should look like this:

Click on Find Next to find the next text in the document that has italics applied.

For each word that is in italics, then go to the Find and Replace panel in Affinity and type into the Find field the word or a phrase that includes the word that will make it easy to find. Click on the Find option.

You should see a listing of results that match:

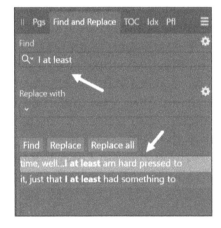

Click on the one you want.

Affinity will take you to that page in the document and highlight the text you searched for. If the search term was the text that needed to be italicized, you can just click on the slanted I in the dynamic menu or use Ctrl + I to apply italics to that search result.

Otherwise, click into the document, select the text you want to italicize, and then apply italics to it.

It used to be that the search function didn't work with apostrophes so you couldn't search for "I'd call" or something like that, but I just tested it and it looks like that issue is now fixed.

When you're done, in Word you need to return your search function to its regular state. So click into the Find What box and use Ctrl + I two more times to return it to a search that doesn't require the text to be italicized before you close the dialogue box.

Repeat for bolded text or any other uniquely formatted text that you need to adjust for.

As I mentioned above, italics do take up a little less space than regular text, so be sure to check when you add italics or bolding to text in a paragraph that it doesn't shift things around.

If it does, I either visually check to make sure it didn't create any new orphans or widows or I use Tracking to expand things just enough to put the lines back to what they were.

TIDYING UP

After you've formatted all of your text and applied your master pages, chances are at the end you'll run into one of two issues.

The first issue, and for me the more common outcome when formatting novels, is that when Affinity first flowed your text for you it flowed it to more pages than you actually need. My paragraph formatting takes up less space than the RTF or Word document formatting that I bring in.

So I get to the last page of text and I have something that looks like this in the Pages section of the Pages panel:

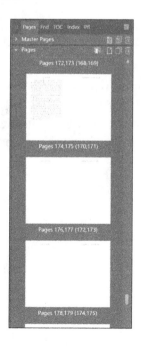

There are a lot of blank pages there that I don't need. To delete blank pages, select them by clicking on the first one, holding down shift, and clicking on the last one.

And then right-click and choose Delete [X] Pages from the dropdown menu where X is the number of selected pages:

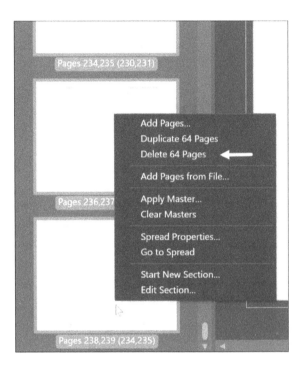

That will delete all of those pages for you.

With non-fiction, I usually have the opposite problem because I use a lot of images and when I insert those images that pushes my text down the page until ultimately I get to the end and have something that looks like this:

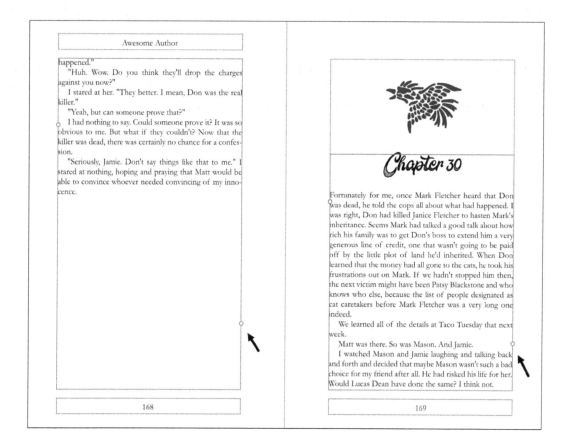

It's a little hard to see, but there is a red circle along the right edge of the text frames. It's going to be on the edge of every text frame in the document when this happens. What that is saying is that there is more text than can be fit into the available text frames.

The solution is to simply reflow your text once more. So click on that little circle on the last page in your document to turn it into an arrow, and then Shift and click on the arrow to flow your text.

Now, one thing to be careful about with this is that if you have a lot of text hidden back there, you want to make sure to change that last page's master page to the Text and Text master page first. (Or whatever your most common master page layout is.) Otherwise Affinity will flow to whatever the current master page layout is for those last two pages, in this case a Text and Chapter Start master page.

I deliberately created this scenario so only had one page for it to flow to, so it doesn't really matter. But I sometimes have thirty pages to flow and then it does.

Ctrl + Z, Undo, is your friend if you mess that up. Just undo, change the last page layout, and then try again.

You can also select that range of pages that Affinity added and then right-click and choose to Apply Master to all of them if you accidentally use the wrong master page layout. Problem is, that likely won't be the same number of pages required and you'll have to then delete pages or reflow again.

ABOUT THE AUTHOR PAGE

Okay. Assuming you've finished with the main body of your document, there's just one more master page to add (for our simplified layout), the About the Author page.

In this current example, my novel ends on the left-hand page, so I just need to change that last thumbnail's master page to Text and About the Author:

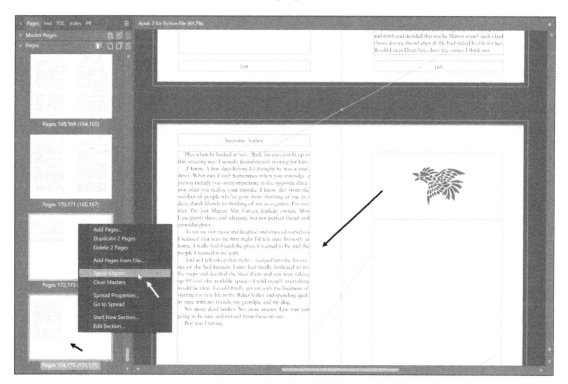

For some reason, in my case, when I did this the text flowed to the about the author page and not the last page on the left-hand side of the spread. If that happens to you, just fix the flow. (Click on the arrow from the right-hand edge of the text frame on the prior page and click back on that text frame to break the incorrect flow, and then click on the arrow on the right-hand edge of that text frame and click on the left-hand page text frame on the final spread to flow to the correct page.)

(I don't know what will go wrong for you, but expect that something will, which is why I leave these little mentions in here.)

Once that final page spread is working properly, simply click into the text frame on the about the author page and add whatever you want to say about the author.

I just had another glitch here where it insisted on using my accent font even when I applied my text styles to the text. So I had to manually format the text using Garamond. I don't know what caused that. I eventually did get it back to the text style I wanted to use.

Sometimes, things are just glitchy and you have to work around them. Sometimes that's user error (me in this case), sometimes it's a computer issue, and sometimes it's going to be the program you're working in. I usually just find a way around unless it's a fatal issue in which case I go digging for a better solution.

Okay.

Here is our final spread:

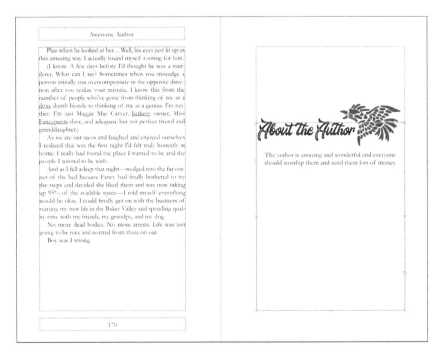

The novel ends on the left-hand page and then the right-hand page is our about the author.

The other outcome you may have at the end of your book is that the text ends on the right-hand page. In that case, you need to add two more pages, so left-click on the final thumbnail, and Add Pages.

You want 2, after the last spread, and the master page should be No Text and About the Author. Click into that right-hand text frame, add your text, and format as needed.

Since we didn't link the about the author text frames to the rest of the document, they are standalone and you can type your text directly into them without worrying about it ending up in the main body of your document.

If that does ever happen where the about the author is part of the rest of the document, you can force your text into that frame by using a frame or page break.

I'll talk about that in the next section because you might need it for other things as well.

OTHER COMMENTS, TIPS, AND TRICKS

FRAME OR PAGE BREAK

There will be times when you want to force text to the next text frame. I do this often with non-fiction but it could come up with fiction as well. To insert a frame break, click where you want the break to happen, then go to Insert→Breaks→Frame Break.

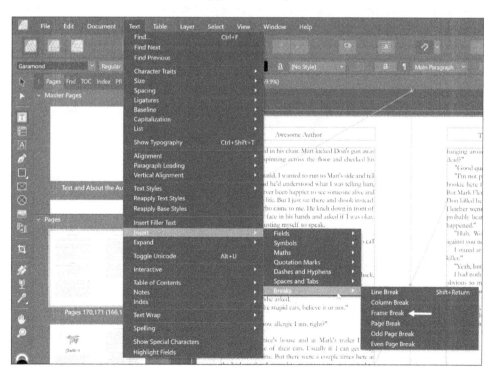

I believe for the setup we used here a Page Break would also work.

One thing to note is that it always inserts an extra line when it does this, so you'll have a blank line and then the rest of the text from the prior frame and will need to delete that blank line. (I don't know why it does that, but it does.)

OTHER FRONT AND BACK MATTER ELEMENTS

In the next book we'll get more complicated about additional front and back matter elements, but I think you can see how to create more master pages if you need them and then add or break text flow between pages as needed. But I just wanted to acknowledge that this is a very basic layout without a lot of bells and whistles. For example, my YA fantasy books include a character guide and terminology guide in the back, and most of my non-fiction have an index and a table of contents.

SPELLCHECK

You may have noticed that Affinity has added red squiggly lines under certain text in my document. That's an indication that it thinks I have spelling errors. I use in the cozies the term "barkery" to refer to a bakery for dogs, for example, so it's flagged each of those uses.

If you go to the Preflight panel, you can see all of the identified issues:

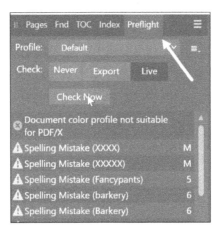

It doesn't just list spelling errors, but for me that's most of it for a novel. You can double-click on any of those entries to go to that page.

Right-click on the entry in your document to see spelling suggestions or to tell Affinity to ignore the error or learn the word.

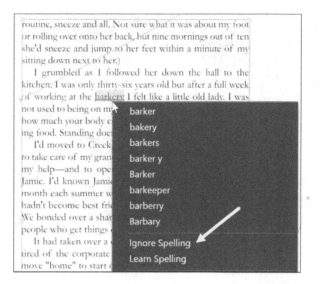

I have a high tolerance for clutter, so I usually don't do anything and just scan the list to make sure my editing passes didn't miss an error. Although I do believe that before it wasn't quite so obvious in the document itself.

PREFLIGHT

In addition to spelling errors, the Preflight panel will identify a number of issues for you. I use it to see when my index or table of contents need updated (a more advanced topic) or when my images are not proportional anymore as well as if I've failed to meet the minimum DPI for print.

If you don't want Preflight to identify a type of error or you do need it to identify something, click on the Preflight panel and then click on the three lines at the end of the tabs listing and choose to Edit Profile. This will bring up the Edit Preflight Profile dialogue box where you can choose what type of warning level something is assigned.

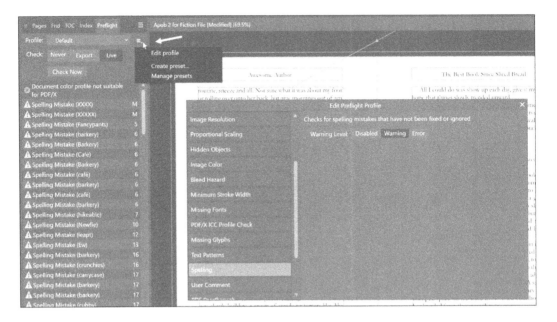

You can also customize some parameters. For example, by default it will alert if your image resolution is below 72 DPI, but I set it to 300 for print.

Also, in Affinity Publisher 2.0 Affinity now tells me that the document color profile is not suitable for a PDF/X file when I have it set to greyscale. You can submit a file to Amazon KDP or IngramSpark that is in color and still have them print it in black and white. But it means that they do the converting on their end.

So if that error bugs you, use a CMYK profile instead of greyscale. So far, I've just ignored it and the books I printed with Amazon and Ingram turned out just fine. But if you're concerned, definitely be sure to order a proof copy to review.

If you have any alerts in preflight, Affinity will warn you about them and ask if you want to look at them before you can export your file, so it's always a good idea to look through it before you attempt to export.

CHANGE IMAGE

This is more something for covers or ads, but you can swap out an image in Affinity. The option that is always available is to go to Window in the top menu and then choose Resource Manager. This will open the Resource Manager dialogue box which will show all of your images in your document.

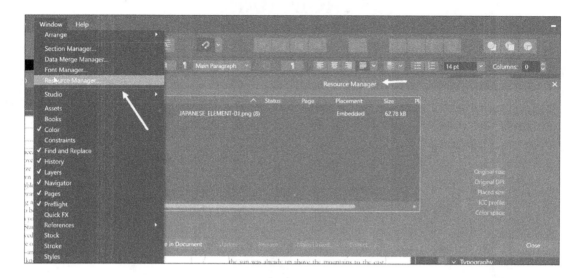

Click on the one you want to replace and then click on the Replace option at the bottom and navigate to the new image you want to use.

Another option is available if you click on the Move Tool and then click on the image on the master page where you inserted it. A Replace Image option will show in the dynamic menu up top.

Any adjustments you made to the prior image after it was inserted into the document will also apply to its replacement. (Rotation is the one that usually catches me out with that.)

OPEN RECENT FILE

I've assumed throughout this that you know the basics of opening and closing Affinity, etc. But do know that under File→Open Recent, you will see a listing of all of your recent Affinity files so that you don't have to go open the file wherever you have it saved. This is pretty standard, but just wanted to mention it.

ZOOM

Zoom can be found under the View menu. You can also use Ctrl + = to Zoom In and Ctrl + - to Zoom Out. I usually find I don't need zoom for print layouts, but just in case. Zoom to Width, Alt + Shift + 0, is also a useful one.

SCROLL BARS

There are scroll bars below the main workspace and on the right-hand side that will let you scroll through your document.

I also often use the wheel on my mouse to do so. Just make sure the cursor is over the main workspace or the thumbnails in the Pages section first, whichever you want to scroll through. (I often start trying to use my mouse to scroll and am on the wrong one.)

EXPORT AS PDF

Okay. Check back through your document one more time to see if it's ready to review. If it is, time to export to a PDF.

Go to File and click on Export. You will likely get this message:

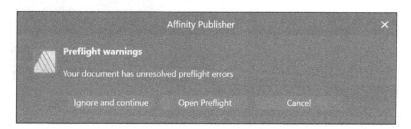

Since I already looked at Preflight, I click on Ignore and Continue. If you choose Open Preflight that will cancel your export.

Next you'll see the Export Settings dialogue box:

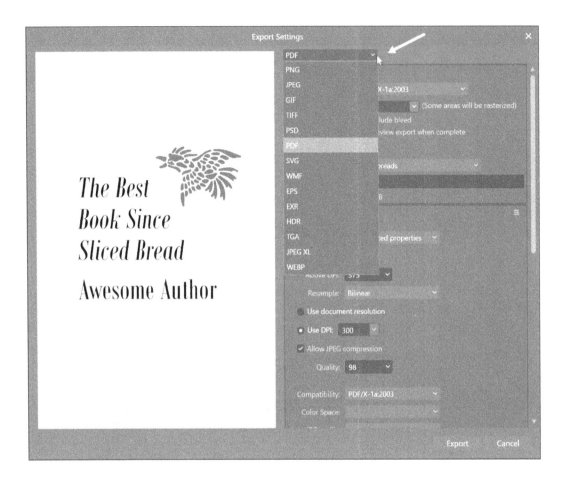

There is a dropdown at the top where you can choose the format to export to. For a print book published through KDP or IngramSpark, you want PDF.

(I use PNG and JPEG for cover or advertising images.)

For a simple novel without a lot of images in it, use the Preset dropdown to choose PDF/X-1a:2003 or PDF/X-3:2003. The IngramSpark file creation guide asks for PDF/X-1a:2001 or PDF/X-3:2002, but those aren't available choices. I've never had an issue submitting with X-1a:2003.

(Note here, I am not a graphic design professional. If this really matters to you, I am not the authority to trust on this.)

I always check the box to preview the export when complete.

This next bit is very, very, very important. Under Area it is going to default to All Spreads.

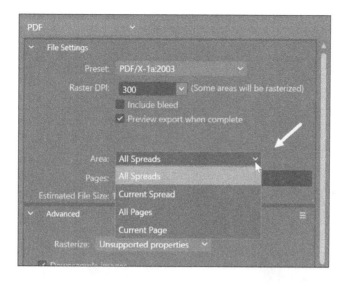

For reviewing the file, that's fine. It's almost better because it lets you see the pages in the appropriate location, left- or right-hand of the page.

But when you are ready to submit to Amazon KDP or to IngramSpark, you must change this setting. It needs to be set to *All Pages*. The PDF you submit should have as many pages as your final book does.

Our example I've been working with has 175 pages showing in the Pages section of the Pages panel. That's what I need to see in my PDF, too. If I see 87 or something like that, I have a problem and will need to re-export.

Another way to check that you exported as All Pages is to look and see if the default view in your PDF viewer shows one page at a time. If you export as All Spreads, the first page will be standalone, but the rest will be paired.

For the final file be absolutely sure that you use All Pages not All Spreads.

You don't need to worry about the Advanced settings for a basic title like this. Just choose that preset for PDF/X-1a:2003, change the dropdown to All Pages, click on Export, and tell Affinity where to save the file.

FINAL DOCUMENT CHECK

I always do one final, thorough document check on the PDF file. Look for the following:

1. Spelling errors in the title page

2. Overlap of text and images in the front matter

3. Missing ISBN (this is why I use XXX in the master page, so I'll notice it)

4. Correct copyright year

5. All chapter starts have the correct master page applied

6. Page 1 of Chapter 1 starts with the page number 1

7. Headers and Footers are correctly spelled and what they should be

8. No header or footer on a page without text

9. No unsightly gaps in text, widows, orphans, really short words ending a paragraph, single lines on a page, etc.

10. All chapter titles have been properly formatted

11. All separators have been properly formatted

12. All first paragraphs have been properly formatted

13. No random blank pages anywhere

14. No header at the top of a chapter start page

15. Headers and footers are at the same height on the left- and right-hand pages.

16. Text is italicized or bolded as needed

17. Images in the document are clear not blurry (if blurry the image may be missing and you may need to link to it again through the Resource Manager or the DPI may not be high enough)

Basically, does it look right? Sometimes this is best seen by printing the document. I worry less about it with novels than with non-fiction titles that have a lot of images, but you should always scroll through at least once. This is also why I always publish to Amazon KDP first when I publish a print book, so I can use their previewer for one final flip through the book.

If you find issues, fix them in Affinity, and then re-export and re-review. Rinse and repeat until the book is ready to go. Once the file is ready, then with both Amazon KDP and IngramSpark you just upload the PDF file along with a cover PDF file and they do the rest.

REUSE AN OLD BOOK

I promised you earlier in this book that you weren't going to have to go through this whole lengthy process every single time you create a book. And that's because once you have one book created, it's pretty easy to delete out the content from that book and reuse the file for a new one.

So let's walk through how to do that now, because there are a few important things to keep in mind if you're going to do this.

Step one, open the old book file and save it as a new document.

Now, go to the Pages section of the Pages panel and find pages 8 and 9. If you added more front matter at some point, it won't be pages 8 and 9 but instead whichever pages represent the third page spread in the main body of your document.

What you want is to keep the beginning of your book and a Text and Text master page to use to flow your text, but the rest of it can go. So click on that third page spread in the main body of your document, hold down Shift, go to the last page spread in your document (the also by for us), click on it, right-click, and Delete [X] Pages.

In my case that was 168 pages.

The next step is to click into the text frame of the main body of your document, use Ctrl + A to select all of the text in the main body (including the 160+ pages of hidden text, because it's still there even if the pages aren't), and Delete. If there were any images in picture frames on those first three pages, delete those, too.

And if your final page spread is not a Text and Text master page, change that over.

Also, go to your Fields panel and update the book title or author name, if needed.

You should now have a seven page (or longer) document that's ready to start editing for the new book you want to create. Go to the title page and update it with your new book information. Make sure the Also By is still accurate or update it in the master pages section. Change the year and ISBN number for the copyright notice. And then dump in the new text of your new title and walk through the process starting with Add and Flow Main Body Text.

Easy enough. You'll already have the master pages we created here as well as the text styles, so it's just a matter of applying them or updating the primary text styles as needed.

CONCLUSION

Okay, there you have it. How to format a basic book that uses a simple accent image using Affinity Publisher 2.0.

Now, a reminder that I am self-taught and am not perfect. So this works for me and has let me format a large number of print books. But if you think I'm wrong or there's a better way to do that or you'd never put the copyright notice on the page I did, that's fair.

Every single time I write a non-fiction book, even one I've written before like this one, I start from scratch because I in the interim have learned new things or may have decided to approach the problem from a different angle. We don't often realize it but we are always learning and growing, so what you and I know today is nothing compared to what we'll know next year.

At the end of the day, if it works, it works, right? I am a firm believer that there is no "only one way to do things" in this world. There's just "did it get you a satisfactory result"? If it did, then great. If not, then you find a new answer.

What we walked through in this book, does that for me and will hopefully do that for you.

Also, if it's too complicated or messy to format your books or you find you don't enjoy it, don't be afraid to switch to a tool like Vellum or Atticus or use D2D's option instead. We each only get so many hours in a day and while a nicely-formatted book does help, the difference between formatted in Affinity and formatted by Vellum probably isn't worth stress and headache if that's what formatting does to you.

Anyway. I hope that won't be the case now that you've read this book. If there's something that was confusing or you get stuck, reach out at mlhumphreywriter@gmail.com.

And if you want to keep going and explore tables of contents, indexes, and inserting images into the body of your document, then continue on to Affinity Publisher 2.0 for Book Formatting Part 2.

APPENDIX A: QUICK TAKES

AUTHOR NAME

FIELD EDIT

Fields panel. Click on field next to Author. Type author name. Enter.

INSERT

Artistic Text Tool. Click on location in document where field should be inserted. Go to Fields panel. Double-click on Author.

BOOK TITLE

FIELD EDIT

Fields panel. Click on field next to Title. Type book title. Enter.

INSERT

Artistic Text Tool. Click on location in document where field should be inserted. Go to Fields panel. Double-click on Title.

DOCUMENT PRESET

CREATE

Use the New dialogue box to specify all document settings. When done, click on the icon with a plus sign next to the name for the document. In the Create Preset dialogue box type a name for the document preset, choose an icon, and choose a Category.

DELETE

Right-click on document preset in the New dialogue box and choose Delete Preset.

MOVE TO NEW CATEGORY

In the New dialogue box, left-click on the document preset in the document preset listing, and drag to the new category.

NEW CATEGORY

In the New dialogue box, at the bottom of the listing of document presets, click on the icon for Create Category. Type the category name in the New Category dialogue box. OK.

RENAME

Right-click on document preset in the New dialogue box and choose Rename Preset. Type new name into Rename Preset dialogue box. OK.

EXPORT

PDF

To export a PDF of your document, go to File→Export, and choose the PDF option. For review purposes, All Spreads is better because it will keep facing pages together in the PDF. For KDP and IngramSpark upload, use All Pages.

IMAGE

DPI

The image DPI will increase as your image size decreases. For print, images should have a minimum DPI of 300. You can change the minimum DPI for the document by going to File→Document Setup→Document and changing the DPI setting there.

INSERT

Place Image Tool. Select image to insert. Open. Image may automatically insert. If not, click and drag in workspace until desired size.

MOVE

Move Tool. Click on image, hold left-click and drag to desired location. Use Snapping to align along edges or center.

REPLACE

Document top menu. Window→Resource Manager. Select image. Replace. Select new image. Open. Close resource manager.

Or. Move Tool selected, click on image, use Replace Image option in dynamic menu. Choose new image. Open

RESIZE

Move Tool. Click on image layer or directly on image if not in a picture frame.

Option A: Transform panel. Lock Aspect Ratio. Change height or width value.

Option B: Click on blue circle in corner and drag at an angle to resize proportionately. Or click on blue circle along any edge to change height or width only. This will skew most images.

WRAP

To have text jump or wrap around an inserted image, click on the image and then use the Show Text Wrap Settings in the top menu to choose the Wrap Style.

MASTER PAGE

ADD NEW

Pages panel. Master Pages section. Right-click on existing master page.

Option A: Choose Insert Master. Click OK to create a new master page that has the basic properties of the existing master page.

Option B: Choose Duplicate to create an exact duplicate of the existing master page.

MOVE

Pages panel. Master Pages section. Left-click on master page and drag. Blue line along edge will show where master page will move to. Release left-click when positioned where wanted.

RENAME

Pages panel. Master pages section. Click on master page thumbnail. Click on name of master page. Type in new name. Enter.

PAGE NUMBER

CHANGE NUMBERING STYLE

Pages panel. Pages section. Right-click on page and choose Edit Section. Click on section name that contains the pages where you want to change the numbering style if not already visible. Choose the new style from the Number Style dropdown menu. Close.

INSERT

Master page. Artistic Text Tool. Click where you want page number placed. Go to top menu, Text→Insert→Fields→Page Number.

RESTART AT 1

Pages panel. Pages section. Right-click on page where you want to restart at 1. Start New Section. (Or Edit Section if one has already been started.) Click button for Restart Page Numbering At. Enter 1. Change numbering style if needed. Close.

PAGES

ADD

Pages panel. Pages section. Right-click on an existing page or page spread. Add Pages. Choose the number of pages to add, whether to insert before or after that location, and choose the master page to use for the inserted pages. OK.

APPLY MASTER PAGE

Pages panel. Pages section. Right-click on the pages where you want to apply the master page. (Be sure that both pages are selected in a two-page spread.) Apply Master. Choose desired master page from dropdown menu. OK.

DELETE

Pages panel. Pages section. Select pages or page spreads that you want to delete. Right-click. Delete X Pages.

SELECT

If you only want to edit one page in a two-page spread, be sure to click on just that side of the page spread. Only that one page should be surrounded by a blue border.

If there is more than page spread that you want to select, click on the first page or page spread at one end of the page range, hold down the shift key and click on the last page or page spread at the other end of the page range.

PANEL

CLOSE

To close a panel either go to the Window menu and click on the panel name or left-click and drag the panel until it is standalone in your workspace and then click on the X in the top right corner.

MOVE OR ANCHOR

Left-click on panel tab and drag to desired location. To anchor, either drag until you see a blue box appear and then release or drag to where other panels are already anchored and add to those tabs.

OPEN

To open a panel go to the Window menu and click on the panel name. Some panels are listed in secondary dropdown menus.

RECOVER FILE

RECOVER FILE

If Affinity ever crashes and closes while you were working on a file, reopen the program and try to reopen the file. Affinity should tell you that there is a recovery version of the file available. Choose to open the recovery version and then check for the last edits you made to determine if any of your work was lost and needs to be redone.

SECTION

CHANGE START PAGE

Pages panel. Pages section. Right-click and Edit Section. In Section Manager, change the "Start On Page".

CREATE

Pages panel. Pages section. Right-click on the page that you want to have start the new section, Start New Section. In Section Manager, assign name if desired and verify page numbering format and whether it should restart or continue.

EDIT

Pages panel. Pages section. Right-click and Edit Section.

DELETE

Pages panel. Pages section. Right-click and Edit Section. In Section Manager, click on the section you want to delete and use the small trash can icon to delete it.

RESTART PAGE NUMBERING

Pages panel. Pages section. Right-click and Edit Section. For the section that needs to restart page numbering, check the box to "restart page numbering at", verify the page number, generally 1, and the number style.

SNAPPING

ENABLE

Go to the horseshoe shaped magnet image in the top center. Click on the dropdown arrow. Check the box next to Enable Snapping.

USE

To use snapping, as you move an object around in your workspace Affinity will show either green or red lines on the workspace when the object is aligned with the edges or center of other objects on the page.

STUDIO PRESET

ADD NEW

Arrange panels as desired. Go to top menu. Window→Studio→Add Preset. Type name. OK.

APPLY

Top menu. Window→Studio. Select desired preset. Or use Ctrl + Shift + [Number] preset for that studio.

DELETE

Window→Studio→Manage Studio Presets. Select preset name. Delete. Close.

RENAME

Window→Studio→Manage Studio Presets. Select preset name. Rename. Type in new name. OK.

SAVE CHANGES

Make desired changes to panel preset arrangement. Window→Studio→Add Preset. Type in exact same name as before. OK. Agree to overwrite old preset.

TEXT

ADD SPACE BETWEEN LINES

Artistic Text Tool. Select paragraph of text. Paragraph panel. Spacing section. Leading dropdown. Choose desired option. Or for multiple lines of the same style, click on Space Between Same Styles and set a value.

ADD SPECIAL SYMBOLS OR CHARACTERS

Artistic Text Tool. Click into workspace where desired. Go to the Glyph Browser panel. (Window→Text→Glyph Browser if not open.) Find desired symbol or character. Double-click on symbol or character to insert.

ALIGNMENT

Artistic Text Tool. Click on the paragraph or select the paragraphs. Dynamic menu choices above workspace. Four images with lines. Align Left, Align Center, Align Right, or dropdown menu for Justify Left, Justify Center, Justify Right, Justify All, Align Towards Spine, Align Away From Spine. Or, to the right of that, dropdown menu for Top Align, Center Vertically, Bottom Align, Justify Vertically.

The horizontal alignment options are also available at the top of the Paragraph panel.

ALL CAPS OR SMALL CAPS

Artistic Text Tool. Select the text to be formatted. Go to Character panel. Typography section. Click on the two capital Ts to apply all caps. Click on the capital T with a smaller capital T to apply small caps. Check your text entries for issues with using a capital letter or lower case letter when working with small caps because the two do look different in small caps.

BOLD

Artistic Text Tool. Select text. Font Style dropdown menu, Ctrl + B, or click on B in top menu.

Or go to Character panel and choose the Strong option from the Character Style dropdown menu at the top or use the Font Style dropdown menu.

Only works if there is a bold version of the font available.

FONT

Artistic Text Tool. Select text. Top menu, left-hand side. Font Family dropdown. Choose font.

Or select text and go to Character panel and use the Font Family dropdown at top.

HYPHENATION

Artistic Text Tool. Select text. Paragraph panel. Hyphenation section. Click on box next to Use Auto-Hyphenation. Change values as needed.

INDENT PARAGRAPH

Artistic Text Tool. Select paragraph. Paragraph panel. Spacing section. Second option on left-hand side. (First Line Indent). Add value.

ITALICS

Artistic Text Tool. Select text. Font Style dropdown menu, Ctrl + I, or click on I in top menu.

Or go to Character panel and choose the Emphasis option from the Character Style dropdown menu at the top or use the Font Style dropdown.

Only works if there is an italic version of the font available.

JUMP IMAGE

Move Tool. Select image. Click on Show Text Wrap Settings option in top menu. In Text Wrap dialogue box choose Jump as desired Wrap Style.

KEEP TOGETHER

Artistic Text Tool. Select second paragraph that you want to keep together. Go to the Paragraph panel. Flow Options section. Check box for Keep With Previous Paragraph.

LINE SPACING (LEADING)

Artistic Text Tool. Select paragraph. Paragraph panel. Spacing section. Change value in Leading dropdown. Default is usually a good place to start.

MOVE TO NEXT PAGE

Click right after the text that's before the text you want to move to the next page. Go to Text→Insert→Break→Frame Break to move the text to the next frame or →Page Break to move to the next page.

ORPHANS REMOVE AUTOMATICALLY

Paragraph panel. Flow Options. Check box for Prevent Orphaned First Lines.

SIZE

Artistic Text Tool. Select text. Top menu, left-hand side. Font Size dropdown. Choose size or type in size.

Or select text and go to Character panel and use the Font Size dropdown at top.

SMALL CAPS

See *All Caps or Small Caps*.

TRACKING

Artistic Text Tool. Select text. Character panel. Positioning and Transform section. Second option in the left-hand column, Tracking. Click arrow for dropdown menu. Choose desired change.

UNDERLINE

Artistic Text Tool. Select text. Ctrl + U or click on the underlined U in top menu.

Or go to Character panel and choose one of the underlined U options from the Decorations section.

WEIGHT

Artistic Text Tool. Select text. Top menu, left-hand side. Font Style dropdown. Choose from available weights for that font.

Or select text and go to Character panel Font Style dropdown at top.

WIDOWS REMOVE AUTOMATICALLY

Paragraph panel. Flow Options. Check box for Prevent Widowed Last Lines.

WRAP AROUND IMAGE

Move Tool. Select image. Click on Show Text Wrap Settings option in top menu. In Text Wrap dialogue box choose Wrap Style.

TEXT FLOW

AUTO FLOW

Pages panel. Pages section. Double-click on last page spread in section. Go to right-hand edge of last text frame in workspace. Click on red circle to see red arrow. Hold down shift key and click on red arrow. Affinity will flow the text to as many page spreads as needed using the same master page spread format as the last one.

FROM ONE TEXT FRAME TO ANOTHER (ADD)

Click on blue arrow along the edge of the first text frame. Click on second text frame.

FROM ONE TEXT FRAME TO ANOTHER (REMOVE)

Click on the blue arrow along the edge of the first text frame. Click back onto the first text frame. If arrow is not visible, click on that text frame first.

TEXT FRAME

CHANGE SIZE

Frame Text Tool or Move Tool. Click on text frame or layer for text frame in Layers panel. Use Transform panel to input specific values or use blue circles around perimeter and left-click and drag.

ALIGN OR POSITION

Frame Text Tool or Move Tool. Left-click on text frame and hold as you drag. Look for red and green alignment lines to center or align to other elements in workspace. (Turn on Snapping if there are no red or green lines.)

INSERT

Frame Text Tool. Click and drag in workspace.

TEXT STYLE

APPLY

Artistic Text Tool. Select text. Use dropdown menu at top to apply style. Or go to Text Styles panel and click on desired style. Or use shortcut if one is associated with the style.

BASED ON OTHER STYLE

To base a text style off of another style, first apply the existing text style. Next, make any edits to create the new style. Finally, save as new style.

KEYBOARD SHORTCUT

For a new style, add a keyboard shortcut in the Style section of the Create Paragraph Style dialogue box where it says Keyboard Shortcut. (Don't type the description, just use the shortcut when you're clicked into the box.) For an existing style, go to the Text Styles panel, right-click on the style name, Edit [Style Name], and then in the Style section of the Edit Text Style dialogue box, add the keyboard shortcut.

NEW

Artistic Text Tool. Select text. Format text. Style dropdown in top menu. New Style. Give style a name and keyboard shortcut if desired. OK.

UPDATE OR CHANGE

Artistic Text Tool. Select text with style to be updated. Make edits. Click on Update Paragraph Style option to the right of the style dropdown menu in the top menu area.

Or, go to Text Styles panel, right-click on text style name, Edit [Style Name], make edits in Edit Text Style dialogue box, OK.

APPENDIX B: CREATE A BOOK
FROM AN EXISTING FILE

1. Delete out any old text from the main body of the existing file and delete all pages except the front matter, first chapter start page, and the first Text and Text page.

2. If you want to use different fonts in your document than are used in the existing file, change the fonts for the relevant text styles. If your document is set up with primary and secondary text styles then you only need to change the primary text style for each font.

3. Replace the image(s) in the document or delete the images from the master pages, if needed.

4. After you've replaced any image, make sure it is still positioned properly on each master page.

5. Edit the text on the Title page to reflect the correct book title.

6. Edit the text on the Also By page to reflect the correct series name(s) and title name(s).

7. Edit the text on the Copyright page to show the copyright year, copyright name, and ISBN for the title.

8. Go to the Fields panel and edit the Author and Title fields to show the correct author name and book title.

9. Paste in the main body text of your document.

10. If your text imported with an assigned style or styles, you can use find and replace to change the assigned styles to the ones you need. Otherwise, apply the main body text style for now.

11. Flow your text by Shift + clicking on the red arrow on the right-hand edge of the right-hand text box of the last page which should be a Text and Text page.

12. Assign chapter header and paragraph text styles to the first page of the main body of the book. Double-check that the document looks good. That all images are placed properly, chapter starts are where you want them, paragraphs are formatted as desired, etc. If not, fix those issues in your master pages or text styles before proceeding.

13. Walk through your main body text and assign chapter header, first paragraph, and section break formatting to the text as needed. Also change the master page assigned for each spread when needed. And fix any widows, orphans, one-line chapter ends, etc.

14. Italicize or bold text that was overwritten when the text styles were applied.

15. At the end of the document you may need to either reflow the text again to cover all of your text and/or there may be extra pages that weren't used that need to be deleted.

16. Add your back matter. At a minimum this should include an About the Author page.

17. Export to PDF.

18. Review the PDF file and verify that all pages exported and look as expected. Specifically check headers, footers, paragraph formatting, master page assignment, chapter header and section break formatting, front matter, and back matter. Also check for single-line chapter endings, widows, orphans, short words at the end of paragraphs, and too much white space in justified paragraphs.

19. For any issues, fix them in the Affinity file and then re-export and re-review. Repeat as needed.

20. When final, Export to PDF (PDF X-1a:2003 should work for most purposes) being sure to change the Area selection to All Pages from All Spreads. The PDF should be ready to upload for printing.

Index

ABOUT THE AUTHOR

M.L. Humphrey is a self-published author with both fiction and non-fiction titles published under a variety of pen names.

You can reach her at:

mlhumphreywriter@gmail.com

or at

www.mlhumphrey.com